Keynote

3A COMBO SPLIT

Paul Dummett
Helen Stephenson
Lewis Lansford
Richard Walker
and Ingrid Wisniewska

NATIONAL GEOGRAPHIC LEARNING | CENGAGE Learning

Australia • Brazil • Mexico • Singapore • United Kingdom • United States

NATIONAL GEOGRAPHIC LEARNING | CENGAGE Learning

Keynote Combo Split 3A
Paul Dummett, Helen Stephenson, Lewis Lansford, Richard Walker, and Ingrid Wisniewska

Publisher: Andrew Robinson

Executive Editor: Sean Bermingham

Senior Development Editor: Derek Mackrell

Associate Development Editors: Melissa Pang, Yvonne Tan

Director of Global Marketing: Ian Martin

Senior Product Marketing Manager: Caitlin Thomas

IP Analyst: Kyle Cooper

IP Project Manager: Carissa Poweleit

Media Researcher: Leila Hishmeh

Senior Director of Production: Michael Burggren

Senior Production Controller: Tan Jin Hock

Manufacturing Planner: Mary Beth Hennebury

Compositor: MPS North America LLC

Cover/Text Design: Brenda Carmichael

Cover Photo: Cyclists reflected in Main-Danube Canal near Nurnberg: © Gerd Ludwig/ National Geographic Creative

Combo Split 3A with My Keynote Online:
ISBN-13: 978-1-337-10896-6

Combo Split 3A:
ISBN-13: 978-1-337-10880-5

National Geographic Learning
20 Channel Center Street
Boston, MA 02210
USA

Cengage Learning is a leading provider of customized learning solutions with office locations around the globe, including Singapore, the United Kingdom, Australia, Mexico, Brazil, and Japan. Locate your local office at **international.cengage.com/region**

Cengage Learning products are represented in Canada by Nelson Education, Ltd.

Visit National Geographic Learning online at **NGL.cengage.com**
Visit our corporate website at **www.cengage.com**

Printed in the United States of America
Print Number: 01 Print Year: 2016

Contents

Featured TEDTALKS

1 Mark Bezos
A life lesson from a volunteer firefighter

2 Derek Sivers
How to start a movement

3 Kenneth Shinozuka
My simple invention, designed to keep my grandfather safe

4 Margaret Gould Stewart
How giant websites design for you (and a billion others, too)

5 Haas and Hahn
How painting can transform communities

6 Melissa Marshall
Talk nerdy to me

Scope and Sequence

	LESSON A		LESSON B	
UNIT	**VOCABULARY**	**LISTENING**	**LANGUAGE FOCUS**	**SPEAKING**
 **1 Making a Difference**	Collocations to describe giving help	**Inspiring dreams** *Peter Draw, artist*	**Function** Talking about present and past actions **Grammar** Review of present and past tenses	Talking about ways to help
 **2 Trends**	Collocations to describe trends	**Analyzing trends** *Tara Hirebet, trend expert*	**Function** Talking about future trends **Grammar** Review of future tenses: *will* and *going to*	Describing future trends
 **3 Improving Lives**	Healthcare	**My health routine** *Kate Chong, sports enthusiast*	**Function** Talking about cause and effect **Grammar** Conjunctions for cause and effect	Talking about healthcare tech
	PRESENTATION 1 Talking about how you can make a difference			
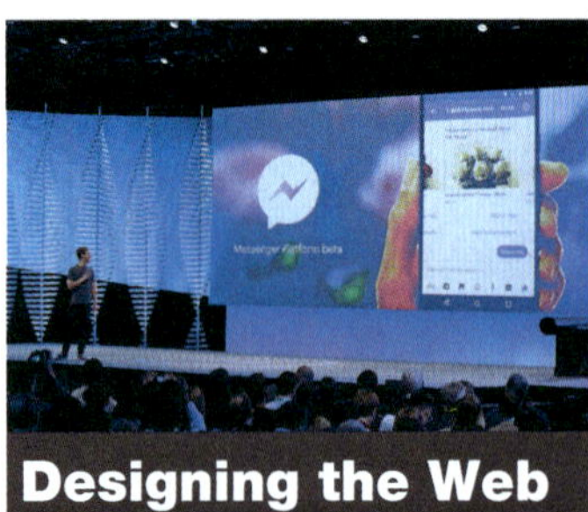 **4 Designing the Web**	Website features	**Designing websites** *Carrie Cousins, web designer*	**Function** Comparing products and services **Grammar** Comparatives and superlatives, *(not) as … as, (very) different from …, … the same as …*	Making decisions based on user reviews
 **5 Community Builders**	Words for talking about communities	**Creating green spaces** *Martín Andrade, entrepreneur*	**Function** Talking about how places have changed **Grammar** The passive voice	Describing changes in my community
 **6 Clear Communication**	Communication collocations	**Communication styles** *Neil Anderson, teacher trainer*	**Function** Talking about communication preferences **Grammar** Verb patterns with *-ing* and infinitive	Communication methods
	PRESENTATION 2 Suggesting a way to improve communication among residents and strengthen the sense of community in your neighborhood			

LESSON C	LESSON D		LESSON E	
READING	**TED TALK**	**PRESENTATION SKILLS**	**COMMUNICATE**	**WRITING**
Food rescue mission	**A LIFE LESSON FROM A VOLUNTEER FIREFIGHTER** *Mark Bezos*	Helping your audience visualize	People who have made a difference	Writing about someone who has made a difference in your life
Identifying trends	**HOW TO START A MOVEMENT** *Derek Sivers*	Commenting on visuals	Consumer trends	Making predictions about a product or service
The challenge of Alzheimer's	**MY SIMPLE INVENTION, DESIGNED TO KEEP MY GRANDFATHER SAFE** *Kenneth Shinozuka*	Opening with interesting facts	Innovative healthcare solutions	Writing a letter about a tech solution for a healthcare issue
Website design on a giant scale	**HOW GIANT WEBSITES DESIGN FOR YOU (AND A BILLION OTHERS, TOO)** *Margaret Gould Stewart*	Asking the audience questions	Improving user experiences	Writing a review of your cell phone
Barefoot College	**HOW PAINTING CAN TRANSFORM COMMUNITIES** *Haas and Hahn*	Ending with a hope for the future	A neighborhood survey	Writing a letter about improving your neighborhood
Communication in the digital age	**TALK NERDY TO ME** *Melissa Marshall*	Engaging with your audience	Explaining a topic of interest	Writing what you learned about a topic

Welcome to Keynote!

In this book, you will develop your English language skills and explore great ideas with an authentic TED Talk. Each unit topic is based around a TED speaker's main idea.

In Unit 3, Kenneth Shinozuka shares his ideas for using sensor technology to improve the lives of people with Alzheimer's and those who care for them.

LISTENING AND SPEAKING

- Practice listening to real people talking about the unit topic. Real-life people featured in this book include an artist, an entrepreneur, and a guidance counselor.
- Develop your **speaking confidence** with a model conversation and guided speaking tasks.

See pages 39, 41

VOCABULARY AND GRAMMAR

- In each unit, you'll learn key words, phrases, and grammar structures for talking about the unit topic.
- Build **language and visual literacy skills** with real-life information—in Unit 3, you'll learn about how technology can help improve personal health care.

See pages 38, 40

READING

- Develop your **reading and vocabulary skills** with a specially adapted reading passage. In Unit 3, you'll learn about the challenge of dealing with Alzheimer's disease.
- The passage includes several words and phrases that appear later in the TED Talk.

See pages 42–44

VIEWING

- Practice your viewing and **critical thinking** skills as you watch a specially adapted TED Talk.
- Notice how TED speakers use effective language and **communication** skills to present their ideas.

See pages 45–47

COMMUNICATING AND PRESENTING

- Use your **creativity** and **collaboration skills** in a final task that reviews language and ideas from the unit.

See page 48

- Build your **speaking confidence** further in a Presentation task (after every three units).

See page 49

WRITING

- Communicate your own ideas about the unit topic in a controlled writing task.

See page 48

- Develop your **writing and language skills** further in the **Keynote Workbook** and online at **MyKeynoteOnline**.

What is TED?

TED has a simple goal: to spread great ideas. Every year, hundreds of presenters share ideas at TED events around the world. Millions of people watch TED Talks online. The talks inspire many people to change their attitudes and their lives.

SPREADING IDEAS WORLDWIDE

Over 10,000 TEDx events in 167 countries

Over 2,200 TEDTALKS recorded

TEDTALKS translated into 105 languages

Over 1,000,000,000 views of TEDTALKS at TED.com

1 Making a Difference

> “Not every day is going to offer us a chance to save someone's life, but every day offers us an opportunity to affect one.”

Mark Bezos
Volunteer firefighter, TED speaker

UNIT GOALS

In this unit, you will ...

- talk about how people can make a difference.
- read about how simple actions can help others.
- watch a TED Talk about a life lesson from a volunteer firefighter.

WARM UP

▶ 1.1 Watch part of Mark Bezos's TED Talk. Answer the questions with a partner.

1 What situation is Bezos describing? What was he asked to do?

2 Look through the unit. What are some ways we can help people?

Volunteers unloading food supplies in Yogyakarta, Indonesia

1A Everyday heroes

VOCABULARY Giving help

A 1.2 Complete the sentences. Circle the most suitable words. Then listen and check your answers.

1 Even small acts of kindness can (**take care of** / **make a difference to**) people's lives.

2 When friends go through difficult times, it's important to (**be there for** / **make an impact on**) them.

3 The work of great people, like Nelson Mandela, (**helps out** / **makes an impact on**) millions of people's lives.

4 Doctors and nurses (**inspire** / **take care of**) sick and injured people.

5 Scientists can (**be there for** / **inspire**) positive changes in the world through their work.

6 Charities often need volunteers to (**help out at** / **inspire**) their events.

B Work with a partner. Discuss these questions.

1 What are some jobs or professions in which people help others? What do they involve? Would you like to do any of them?

2 When was the last time you helped take care of someone? What did you do?

3 Is there someone who inspires or has inspired you?

One job in which people help others is …

I would be interested in being a(n) … because …

LISTENING Inspiring dreams

Expressing beliefs and wishes

Here are some common expressions we can use to talk about our wishes.

I hope to … *I want to …* *It's my dream to …*

A ▶ 1.3 Watch artist Peter Draw talk about his work. What are some of the ways he affects people's lives?

- ☐ He teaches art to children.
- ☐ He designs homes for people.
- ☐ He raises money for sick children.
- ☐ He uses art to help disaster survivors.

Peter Draw with a student in Fukushima, Japan

B ▶ 1.3 Watch again. Complete the information about the lessons Peter Draw has learned.

1 It's important to work hard and ______________________.

2 Every little thing we do can ______________________.

3 Don't wait to ______________________.

C **CRITICAL THINKING**

Reflecting How does Peter Draw feel his work is helping to make a difference in the world?

SPEAKING Talking about helping people

A ▶ 1.4 What did Speaker B help with?

A: Do people often ask you for help?

B: Yeah, sometimes. People usually ask me to repair things, because I'm good at it.

A: So have you helped anyone recently?

B: Yeah, my brother. He needed help with his bicycle because the wheel was damaged.

A: When was that?

B: It was last month.

A: And how did it go?

B: I replaced the wheel for him, and he was really happy!

B Practice the conversation with a partner.

C Work with a partner. Talk about some ways you have helped other people. Use the expressions in blue above to help you.

People usually ask me to help them move house because I have a big van.

Have you helped anyone move recently?

1B Making an impact

LANGUAGE FOCUS Discussing ways to contribute

A 1.5 Read the information. Give some examples of how you can do these things.

B 1.6 Listen to the conversation. What did the woman at the grocery store do to help the elderly couple?

C 1.7 Watch and study the language in the chart.

Talking about present and past actions

Peter Draw uses art to make a difference in people's lives.
I'm making dolls to sell at a charity fair.
Many scientists are working to make the world a better place.

The volunteers cleaned up the beach.
I helped an injured cat when I was volunteering at an animal shelter.
The nurses were talking to my grandfather when I visited him at the hospital.

The Internet has changed the way we help people in need.
Governments around the world have signed an agreement to fight climate change.

For more information on **present and past tenses**, see Grammar Summary 1 on pages 182–183.

D ▶ 1.6 Listen to the conversation in **B** again. Complete the sentences from the conversation.

1 "I ____________ in line, and there ____________ a few people in front of me."

2 "An elderly couple ____________ at the front of the line."

3 "The elderly couple ____________ pretty surprised at first, and ____________ to take her money."

E Complete the sentences. Circle the correct words.

1 It (**became** / **has become**) really easy to raise money for a good cause online. It (**took** / **is taking**) me just a few minutes to learn how to use a fundraising website yesterday.

2 Whenever I (**went** / **go**) to the recycling center, I see lots of people who (**are recycling** / **were recycling**) their trash.

3 A few weeks ago, I (**am teaching** / **taught**) my grandmother how to make video calls.

4 People (**are beginning** / **begin**) to show more concern for the environment.

5 (**Have you ever done** / **Were you doing**) volunteer work for a charity? I (**do** / **did**) last year, and I (**thought** / **have thought**) it was a great experience.

F ▶ 1.8 Complete the information using the correct form of the words in parentheses. Then listen and check your answers.

There [1] ____________ (**be**) lots of small things we can do to make a difference in people's lives. In 2010, 12-year-old Blare Gooch [2] ____________ (**watch**) TV when he [3] ____________ (**see**) a news program about the Haiti earthquake. On it, a young boy was crying. Blare [4] ____________ (**can't**) stop thinking about what he had seen, and wanted to help in some way. He thought of an idea to collect teddy bears for the children in Haiti. He [5] ____________ (**start**) a project called Blare's Bears for Haiti. Through Facebook, he got many schools to [6] ____________ (**donate**) bears. Blare managed to collect 25,000 bears for Haiti. "It doesn't really matter how small or old you are," he says. "If you're young and think you can't make a big difference in the world, well, you actually can."

Blare Gooch with all the bears he has collected

SPEAKING Talking about ways to help

Work with a partner. Look at the infographic on page 16. Then discuss these questions.

1 Which ideas would you like to try? Why?

2 Which ideas do you think are the most helpful?

3 Can you think of other ideas to add to the list?

> I want to recycle trash. It's important for everyone to help make our environment better.

> I think showing more appreciation to people around you can make a big difference in people's lives.

1C Food rescue mission

PRE-READING Skimming

Skim the article. How does Robert Lee help make a difference in his city?

1.9

When you hear the word *hero*, you may think of someone like Mahatma Gandhi, who **devoted** his life working for his country's independence. But there are also many "everyday" heroes—they may not create change on a global scale, but they do what they can to help make a difference in people's lives. Everyday heroes are normal people who are **passionate** about making the world a better place. One such person is Robert Lee.

Lee grew up in New York City. As his family was not rich, he learned from a young age the importance of **minimizing** food wastage. When he was in college, he was part of a student group that delivered leftover food to homeless shelters. This experience made him realize how serious the problem of food wastage actually was.

After graduating from New York University, Lee and a college friend created a nonprofit[1] organization called Rescuing Leftover Cuisine. Its purpose is to collect unsold food from restaurants and deliver it to homeless shelters and food kitchens. Volunteers pick up food from restaurants around the city and distribute it to those in need.

The process is simple. Using an app developed by Lee and his team, restaurants report the amount of leftover food that they have each day, and then volunteers sign up for delivery slots. The delivery routes are usually short, so volunteers can deliver the food they've collected simply by walking from the restaurants to the shelters. Lee believes this is a very efficient method of delivery.

To date, Lee and his team have successfully rescued over 150,000 kilograms of food, serving almost 300,000 meals to people who need them. Lee has shown how we can take small actions to improve the lives of people around us. A simple idea or action may sometimes seem **insignificant**, but it may have an impact greater than you can imagine. But Lee says that his work isn't over: "It's just the beginning. The need is so great, and there's just so much demand. With more restaurants, who knows how much more we can do."

[1] **nonprofit:** *adj.* not working with the aim of making money

Robert Lee and a group of volunteers collecting food

UNDERSTANDING MAIN IDEAS

What is the main purpose of the passage?

a to explain how Robert Lee got the idea for his organization

b to show an example of how regular people can make a difference

c to explore the problem of food waste in restaurants and households

UNDERSTANDING A SEQUENCE

How does Rescuing Leftover Cuisine work? Order the stages from 1 to 6.

_____ A volunteer agrees to take on the delivery job.

_____ A restaurant is given an app that Lee's team developed.

_____ People in need receive food from the volunteer.

_____ The restaurant reports how much food it has left at the end of the day.

_____ The volunteer picks up unsold food from the restaurant.

_____ The volunteer walks to a homeless shelter with the leftover food.

BUILDING VOCABULARY

A Match the words in blue from the passage to their definitions.

1 devoted ○	○ unimportant
2 passionate ○	○ reducing
3 minimizing ○	○ having strong feelings or beliefs
4 insignificant ○	○ gave all or most of one's effort or time

B Complete the sentences with the correct form of the words in **A**.

1 Many researchers have ____________________ their lives to finding a cure for cancer.

2 Countries need to work together in order to ____________________ the impact of climate change.

3 People who are ____________________ about their jobs tend to work hard and do well.

4 We should all do what we can to help others. No contribution is ____________________.

C **CRITICAL THINKING**

Reflecting Work with a partner. Look at the infographic on page 19. How do you think so much food gets wasted?

Food sometimes gets wasted when we …

Sometimes at the supermarket ...

1D A life lesson from a volunteer firefighter

TEDTALKS

MARK BEZOS works for a charity organization, Robin Hood, which fights **poverty** in New York City. He's also a **volunteer** firefighter in Westchester County, New York, where he lives. Mark Bezos is continuously amazed and motivated by the **acts** of heroism—big and small—that he sees every day.

Mark Bezos's idea worth spreading is that every act of **generosity** matters—even the small ones.

PREVIEWING

Read the paragraphs above. Match each **bold** word to its meaning. You will hear these words in the TED Talk.

1 the state of being extremely poor ____________

2 the quality of being kind and helpful ____________

3 someone who does a job for no pay ____________

4 things done or achieved ____________

VIEWING

A ▶ 1.10 Watch Part 1 of the TED Talk. Choose the correct options.

1 In Bezos's town, there's _____.

  a a lack of skilled firefighters

  b a lack of volunteer firefighters

  c a team of professional firefighters

2 Which word best describes how Mark Bezos felt about his first fire?

  a excited b nervous c worried

3 The woman was probably _____ when the fire started.

  a sleeping b cooking c taking a bath

B ▶ **1.11** Watch Part 2 of the TED Talk. Put the events in the order they happened.

a Bezos carried the shoes downstairs and gave them to the homeowner.

b The homeowner sent a letter thanking the firefighters.

c The captain asked Bezos to go into the house and bring back some shoes.

d The captain asked the other volunteer to rescue a dog from inside the house.

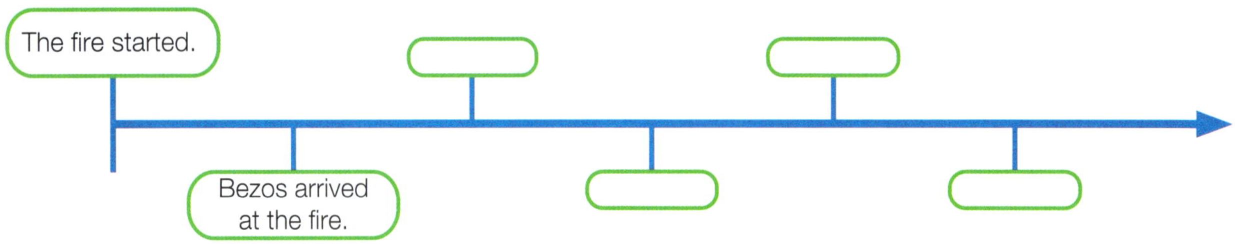

C ▶ **1.12** Watch Part 3 of the TED Talk. Discuss these questions with a partner.

1 What has Mark Bezos learned from the acts of kindness, courage, or generosity that he has seen?

2 Mark Bezos's message to his audience is "Don't wait." What does he mean by this?

D **CRITICAL THINKING**

Inferring Work with a partner. Why do you think Bezos refers to the other firefighter as Lex Luthor (Superman's enemy)? How do you think he really feels about the other volunteer?

Robin Hood volunteer Jasmine Wood reading to a group of children who live in a shelter in New York

VOCABULARY IN CONTEXT

A ▶ 1.13 Watch the excerpts from the TED Talk. Choose the correct meaning of the words.

B Complete the sentences using the words in the box.

witness to	get in on	assignments	above all

1 To ____________ the online discussion, you can visit the Facebook page.

2 As a volunteer, I'm often ____________ how people's lives can be improved through our help.

3 Employees should be hardworking and skilled in their jobs, but ____________ they should be team players.

4 Working on group ____________ helps people learn teamwork.

PRESENTATION SKILLS Helping your audience visualize

To make your presentation more memorable, help your audience visualize the points you are making. You can do this by:

- giving a demonstration
- telling a story
- using pictures and visuals
- sharing interesting facts or statistics

A ▶ 1.14 Watch part of Mark Bezos's TED Talk. What methods does he use to help his audience visualize?

B ▶ 1.14 Watch again. Complete the sentences.

1 "… she was standing outside in the ____________ rain, under an ____________, in her pajamas, ____________, while her house was in flames."

2 "… off I went—up the ____________, ____________ the hall, ____________ the 'real' firefighters …"

C Work with a partner. What methods would you use to help your audience visualize the following?

1 the problem of food wastage around the world

2 a group of people in our society who need care but are often overlooked

3 how someone has helped make a difference in other people's lives

4 how recycling trash is good for the environment

I'd share facts and data about the amount of food we waste.

1E Touching lives

COMMUNICATE People who have made a difference

A Think of someone you know who has made a difference in your life. It could be someone you know personally—a friend, relative, or teacher—or someone you have read or heard about.

B Write some notes about your experience with the person. Use the questions to help you.

- What has that person done to make an impact on you?
- When was it?
- What changes did it make in your life?
- How did the experience make you feel?
- How did it change your thoughts or actions?

C Work with a partner. Talk about how that person has made a difference in your life.

Describing how people have made an impact

I was inspired to … *He motivated me to …*
It transformed the way I … *He changed my mind about …*

Someone who has made an impact on my life is …

One thing that he did that really made a difference is …

What she did made me realize that …

WRITING Describing a personal experience

Write a paragraph about the person who has made an impact on your life and what you gained from that experience.

Someone who has made a big difference in my life is my teacher. She showed me that …

Students attending class on a "boat school" in Bangladesh

2 Trends

UNIT GOALS

In this unit, you will ...

- talk about consumer and technological trends.
- read about how to identify trends.
- watch a TED Talk about how to start a movement.

WARM UP

▶ 2.1 Watch part of Derek Sivers's TED Talk. Answer the questions with a partner.

1 What is happening in the video Sivers shows? What do you think he is going to talk about?

2 Look through the unit. What examples of trends or movements can you find?

From business trends to the latest fashion, trends can be found all around us.

2A Trends around us

VOCABULARY Describing trends

A ▶ 2.2 Circle the correct words. Then listen and check your answers.

1 The economy is doing very well. It is (**growing** / **shrinking**) fast.

2 The number of young people who smoke is (**increasing** / **decreasing**) because of greater health awareness.

3 I eat out more often these days as the quality of food in many restaurants has (**improved** / **gotten worse**).

4 Unhealthy food choices such as fast food are causing health problems like obesity to become (**less common** / **more widespread**).

5 In 1980, the average age of a person in the United States was 30. Now, it has (**risen** / **fallen**) to nearly 40.

6 The Internet has become a part of people's lives. (**Fewer and fewer** / **More and more**) people are shopping or watching TV programs online.

7 Between 1970 and 2014, more affluent households got even (**poorer** / **richer**); their average earnings increased by 47%.

B Complete the sentences describing trends. Use your own ideas.

1 The number of people who ______________________________ has decreased in the last few years.

2 ______________________________ has improved over time.

3 ______________________________ is/are becoming less common nowadays.

4 These days, fewer and fewer people ______________________________.

5 ______________________________ is/are getting richer.

6 The problem of ______________________________ has become more widespread in the last five years.

C Work with a partner. Do you agree with your partner's statements in **B**? Why or why not?

I agree that the number of people who …

LISTENING Analyzing trends

Summarizing details

To check your understanding of what someone said, you can respond with a summary of his or her ideas.

So you mean …? *So what you're saying is …?*

A ▶ 2.3 Watch trend expert Tara Hirebet talk about the work she does. Check (✓) the things that her job involves.

- ☐ reading magazines, articles, books, and blogs
- ☐ developing advertisements for companies
- ☐ spending time with consumers
- ☐ designing logos for businesses

Tara Hirebet is an expert on consumer trends in Asia.

B ▶ 2.4 Watch the next part of the interview and complete the sentences.

1. Trend spotting helps companies learn about their competitors, ________ preferences, and new forms of ________.
2. Hirebet has done trend spotting for ________, technology departments, and startups.
3. Hirebet helped an international sports brand succeed in the ________ youth market.

C CRITICAL THINKING

Evaluating In which industries is it most important to spot trends? Why?

SPEAKING Talking about trends

A ▶ 2.5 Does Speaker A like music streaming?

A: I just signed up for an account on a music-streaming website.

B: Yeah? Streaming music has become really popular in the last few years. So how do you like it so far?

A: I love it. Especially how easy it is to search for different kinds of music. And the best part is it also gives me good recommendations for other artists to listen to.

B: I know. It's completely changed the way people listen to music.

A: Yeah. It's so much more convenient this way. Anyway, I don't have a lot of space in my apartment to keep CDs.

B Practice the conversation with a partner.

C Work with a partner. What are some trends you have adopted recently? What do you think of them? Use the expressions in blue above to help you.

I just started getting into online shopping.

Really? How do you like it so far?

2B Trends in technology

LANGUAGE FOCUS Discussing future trends

A 2.6 Read the timeline. Give some examples of smart devices that you use.

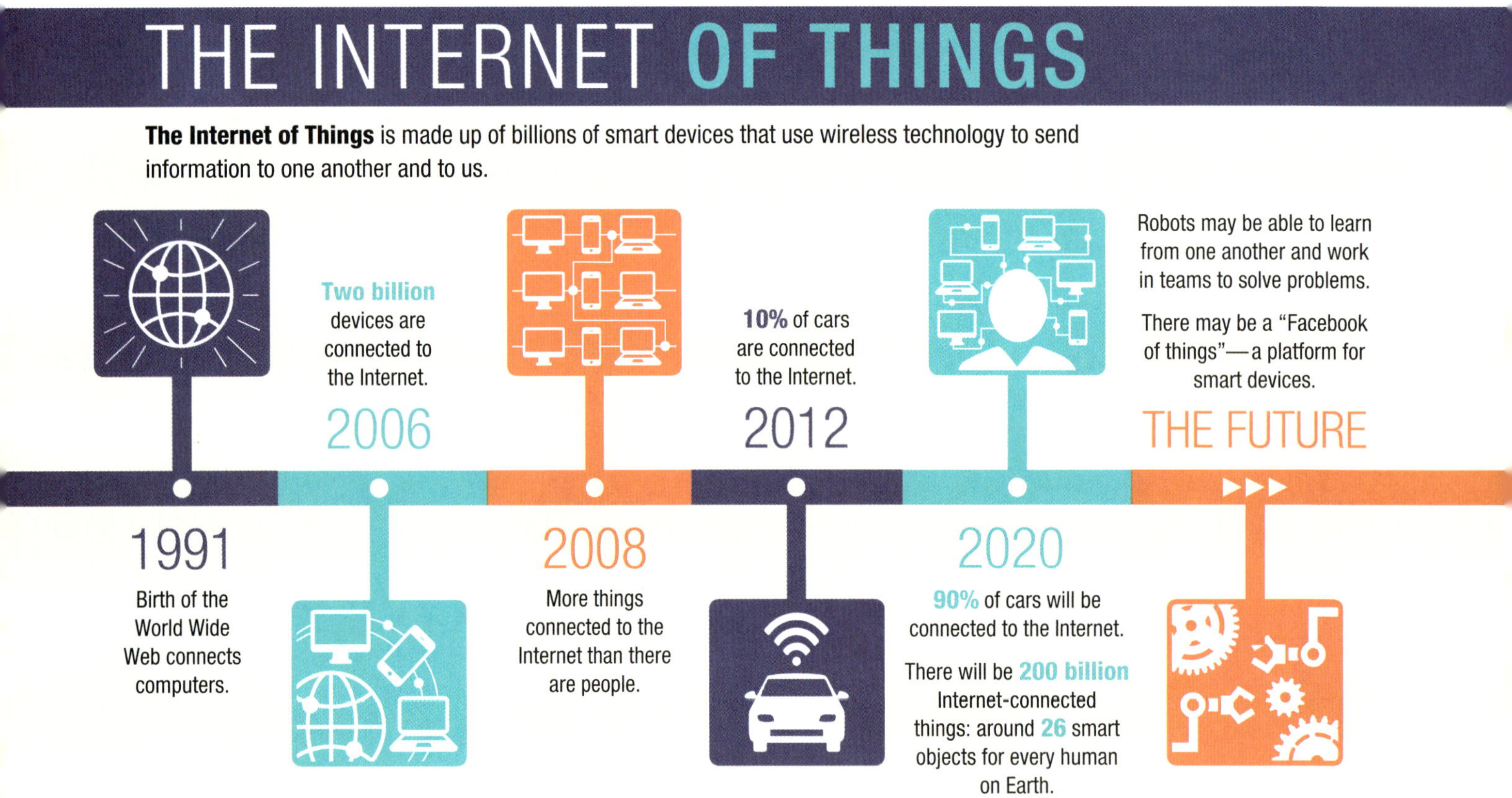

B 2.7 Listen to the conversation. What kind of device does the man want?

The man wants a(n) __________________________________.

C 2.8 Watch and study the language in the chart.

Talking about future trends

I don't think there will be flying cars anytime soon.
Smart devices in the home will become very popular over the next few years.
In twenty years, there won't be many people without smartphones.

Streaming music is going to become the most popular way of listening to music.
Most home appliances are going to be connected to the Internet within five years.
Robots are becoming more common, but they aren't going to replace humans in all professions.

For more information on **will** and **going to**, see Grammar Summary 2 on page 183.

D ▶ 2.7 Listen to the conversation in **B** again. How is the device going to help the man achieve his goal? Complete the sentences from the conversation.

1 "I think ________________ lose weight."

2 "________________ monitor how much fat I'm losing."

3 "I think ________________ for seeing what types of exercises are better for achieving my goals."

4 "I can record the date that I started doing yoga, and ________________ track how well it's helping me lose weight."

E ▶ 2.9 Complete the information. Circle the correct words. Then listen and check your answers.

In the twenty-first century, we [1](**have already seen** / **will see**) three tech revolutions: the rise of broadband, mobile, and the birth of social media. Experts [2](**predict** / **will predict**) that over the next five to ten years, the next tech revolution [3](**connects** / **is going to connect**) billions of devices to the Internet. This is called the Internet of Things—an entire network of devices that are able to "talk" to one another. With this technology, we [4](**will be able to create** / **were creating**) "smart" devices that we can use in our everyday lives. Daniel Burrus, a technology forecaster, believes that there are going to be many new and interesting ways we can use this technology. The Internet of Things [5](**changed** / **is going to change**) the way we work, play, and sleep. Life [6](**will be** / **is**) very different by 2025.

A "smart" home system allows users to control electronic devices in their homes.

F Complete the sentences with your own ideas.

1 Within the next few years, there will be ________________.

2 I think ________________ is/are going to become popular in the next five years.

3 By 2030, there will probably be ________________.

SPEAKING Describing future trends

Work with a partner. Take turns describing and explaining your ideas in **F** above.

I think within the next few years, there will be more "smart" vehicles on the road.

Yeah, I think so, too. Within the next few years, maybe we'll also see other "smart" objects, such as waste bins that can automatically separate trash into different types!

2C Identifying trends

PRE-READING Skimming

Skim the article. Check (✓) the topics that the passage mentions.

- ☐ characteristics of trends
- ☐ jobs in trend spotting
- ☐ trend-spotting tools
- ☐ upcoming business trends

2.10

1 Businesses need to predict change and spot **emerging** trends in order to stay **relevant** and beat the competition. But how can they know what the next big thing is before everyone else?

FADS VERSUS TRENDS

2 One important step in identifying trends is to distinguish[1] them from fads, which don't last long. In 2011, a craze called "planking"—where people photographed themselves lying face down, usually in an odd public place—became popular. However, this turned out to be nothing more than a fad.

3 It's often hard to tell the difference between trends and fads in the early stages. But there are several signs we can look out for. First, trends can make money; businesses should be able to see how they can **take advantage of** a new trend and plan long-term strategies. Second, trends tend to link with one another. For example, the trend of online shopping is related to a bigger trend—the rise of electronic commerce.[2] And third, trends usually appeal[3] to a wide range of people. Planking fails in all three areas, and sure enough, by early 2012, it started to lose popularity.

4 Another way of spotting trends is to observe people's hobbies. The idea for social networking sites like Facebook, Instagram, and Snapchat came from noticing that people like to share photographs or personal information in their free time.

IN SEARCH OF TRENDS

5 The importance of spotting trends has led to a growing industry with a range of new jobs. These vary from individual trend consultants to entire teams of people in large corporations. Social media analysts—a job title that didn't even exist before the mid-2000s—look through huge amounts of data online. Kevin Allocca, whose job is to **analyze** trends on YouTube, spends his day monitoring news headlines and popular videos to help his company look out for industry trends.

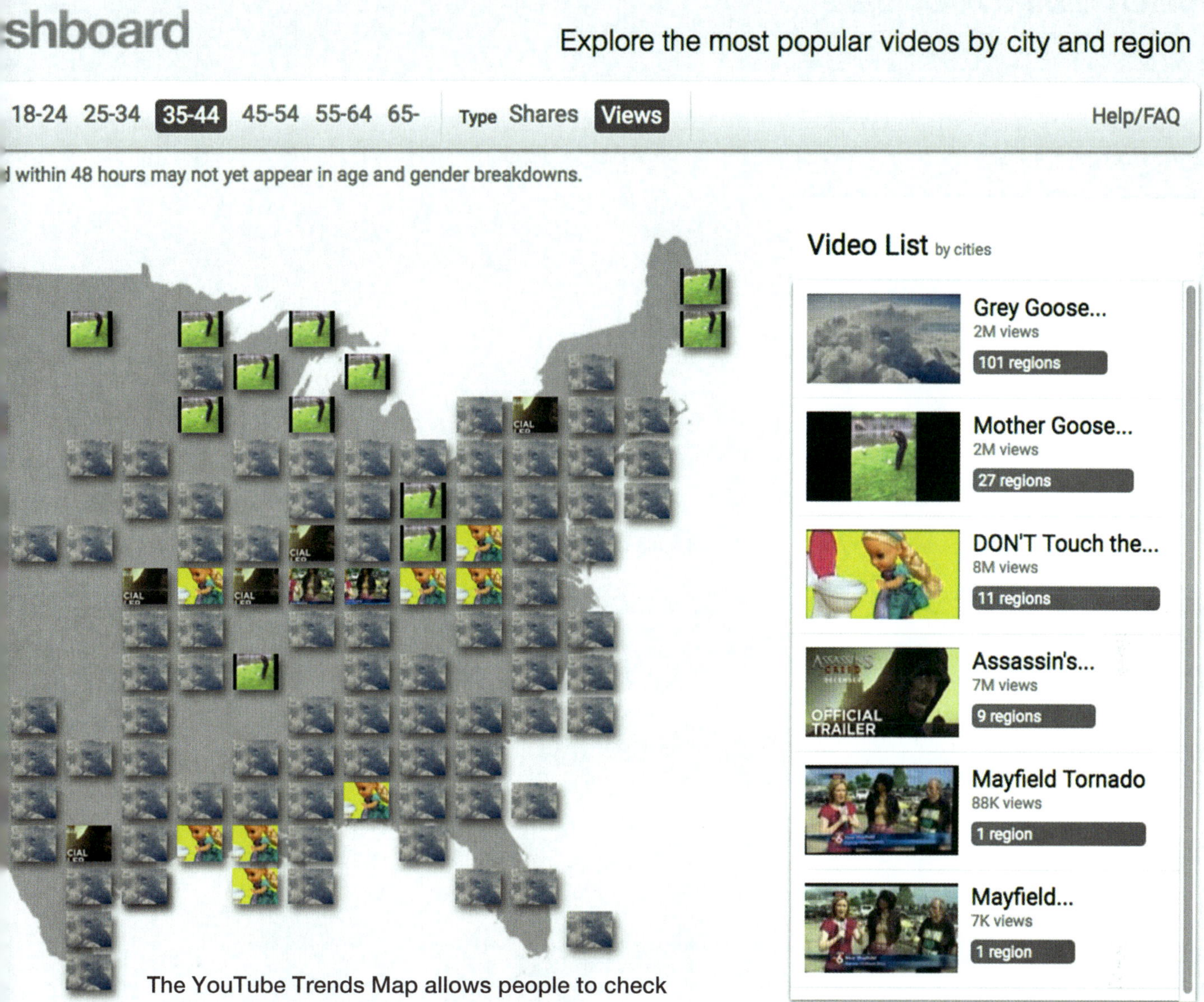

The YouTube Trends Map allows people to check out the most popular videos in their area.

NEW TECHNOLOGY

6 New forms of technology also aid trend spotters. Allocca uses organization tools such as gReader Pro and NetNewsWire to help filter[4] the many websites he monitors every day.

7 Predictive tech analyzes online conversations, blogs, videos, and even photo descriptions. Predictive tech apps search the Web for keywords such as *trend*, *becoming more*, and *recently*, and then compares the data to find common topics.

8 There are also predictive tech websites that encourage trend spotters to work together and submit ideas for new trends. Springwise is a website that allows its members to submit business ideas that they think will work in their city or country. If a member's idea is featured on the website, they receive points that can be exchanged for money.

9 Trend spotting isn't easy, but it is an important skill. Businesses around the world are competing to find the next big thing, and only those that are able to predict and make use of trends will come out on top.

[1] **distinguish:** *v.* to notice a difference between people or things
[2] **commerce:** *n.* the buying and selling of goods and services
[3] **appeal:** *v.* to be liked by people
[4] **filter:** *v.* to separate and remove unwanted materials

UNDERSTANDING MAIN IDEAS

Match each section of the passage to its purpose.

1 Paragraphs 2–4 ○		○ to show how technology can help in predicting trends
2 Paragraph 5 ○		○ to highlight the characteristics of trends
3 Paragraphs 6–8 ○		○ to describe jobs in trend spotting

UNDERSTANDING DETAILS

Complete the concept map.

Identifying trends

- **Characteristics**
  - Trends make 1 ____________.
  - Trends can 2 ____________ with other trends.
  - Trends appeal to a 3 ____________ of people.
- Creation of new 4 ____________
- **Creation of new technology**
  - Predictive tech apps search the 5 ____________ to discover new trends
  - Predictive tech websites get 6 ____________ to work together

BUILDING VOCABULARY

A Match the words in blue from the passage to their definitions.

1 emerging ○		○ growing, upcoming
2 relevant ○		○ study
3 take advantage of ○		○ appropriate
4 analyze ○		○ make use of

B CRITICAL THINKING

Inferring Work with a partner. Which statement below do you think the author would agree with? Why?

1 Jobs like social media analyst show how important trend spotting has become.

2 Predictive technologies have begun to replace human trend spotters.

2D How to start a movement

TEDTALKS

DEREK SIVERS is best known as the founder of CD Baby, one of the first sellers of independent music on the Internet. His company, Wood Egg, advises people on how to build companies.

Derek Sivers's idea worth spreading is that while leaders get the credit for starting a movement, the first followers are often the driving force.

PREVIEWING

Read the sentences. Choose the option that has a similar meaning to each **bold** word. You will hear these words in the TED Talk.

1 You need **guts** to stand up and share your ideas with thousands of people.

a courage **b** ability

2 With the speed of change today, having skilled and resourceful workers is **crucial** to many companies' success.

a useful **b** extremely important

3 Successful business ideas are those that are creative and that **stand out**.

a are practical **b** are noticeable in a crowd

4 A movement often begins with just one **lone** voice.

a single **b** clear

5 When Darwin proposed his theory of evolution, he was **ridiculed** by many people.

a laughed at **b** respected

VIEWING

A 2.11 Watch Part 1 of the TED Talk. Choose the most suitable options.

1 What is the job of the first follower?

a to have the courage to stand out

b to show others how to follow

2 What do you think will happen when the first follower joins?

a Other people will want to join in.

b People will ignore him and the leader.

B ▶ **2.12** Watch Part 2 of the TED Talk. Match the descriptions to the pictures showing the stages of the movement.

a A few more people join.

b People rush to join in so that they can be part of the in-crowd.

c A second follower joins.

d People start to join the group at a faster rate, creating momentum. This is the tipping point.

C ▶ **2.13** Watch Part 3 of the TED Talk. Circle the correct words to complete the advice Sivers gives.

1 The most important thing for a leader to do is to (**have a good idea** / **treat the first followers as equals**).

2 People should not be afraid of (**being the first follower** / **starting their own movement**) when they see someone doing something great.

D CRITICAL THINKING

Inferring Work with a partner. Do you think that people sometimes join a movement or trend because they are afraid of not being part of the in-crowd? Can you think of some examples?

VOCABULARY IN CONTEXT

A ▶ **2.14** Watch the excerpts from the TED Talk. Choose the correct meaning of the words.

B Complete the sentences using the words in the box.

emulate	sit on the fence	nurture	over-glorified

1 People usually ________________ people who inspire them.

2 Schools have a duty to ________________ the talents of all their students.

3 When you need to decide who to vote into government, you can't ________________.

4 Sivers feels that leadership is ________________ because no one becomes a leader without someone else's support.

PRESENTATION SKILLS Commenting on visuals

As you show your visuals, draw the audience's attention to them and highlight the important parts.

A ▶ 2.15 Watch part of Derek Sivers's TED Talk. Check (✓) the expressions he uses in his talk to comment on the visuals.

- ☐ So here's …
- ☐ Now, notice that …
- ☐ Can you see …?
- ☐ Now, there he is …
- ☐ So, pay attention to …
- ☐ So, over the next minute, you'll see …

B Work with a partner. Brainstorm more phrases you could use to draw attention to visuals in a presentation.

C Work with a partner. Choose a video and take turns commenting on the key parts of your video.

> If you look at the man on the right, you'll see that he's taking a photo of himself. Notice that …

2E Predicting trends

COMMUNICATE Consumer trends

A You are going to read about some innovations. **Student A:** Turn to page 165. **Student B:** Turn to page 166.

B Work with a partner. Take turns explaining what the innovations are.

> This is a type of technology that allows people to …

> With this product, people can now …

C Discuss with a partner. Which of these innovations you read or heard about do you think will become more popular in the future? Use the following questions to help you.

Who will the product or service be good for?

What possible applications could there be, and how will people benefit from it?

What other trends would it support?

Describing probability

It's likely to …	*It will probably …*
I think we'll see …	*There's a possibility that …*

WRITING Making a prediction

Write a description of the product or service you read about and your predictions about it.

> Mobile payment technology will probably become a bigger trend in the future. Smartphones have become very common, so people may …

Some smartphones allow users to pay using their mobile phones.

3 Improving Lives

“I really believe that sensors can improve the quality of life of the elderly.”

Kenneth Shinozuka
Inventor, TED speaker

UNIT GOALS

In this unit, you will ...

- talk about healthcare issues and solutions.
- read about the challenges of an aging population.
- watch a TED Talk about how technology can make life better for patients and their caregivers.

WARM UP

▶ **3.1** Watch part of Kenneth Shinozuka's TED Talk. Answer the questions with a partner.

1 What healthcare issue does Shinozuka identify as most serious in the United States?

2 What do you know about this healthcare issue?

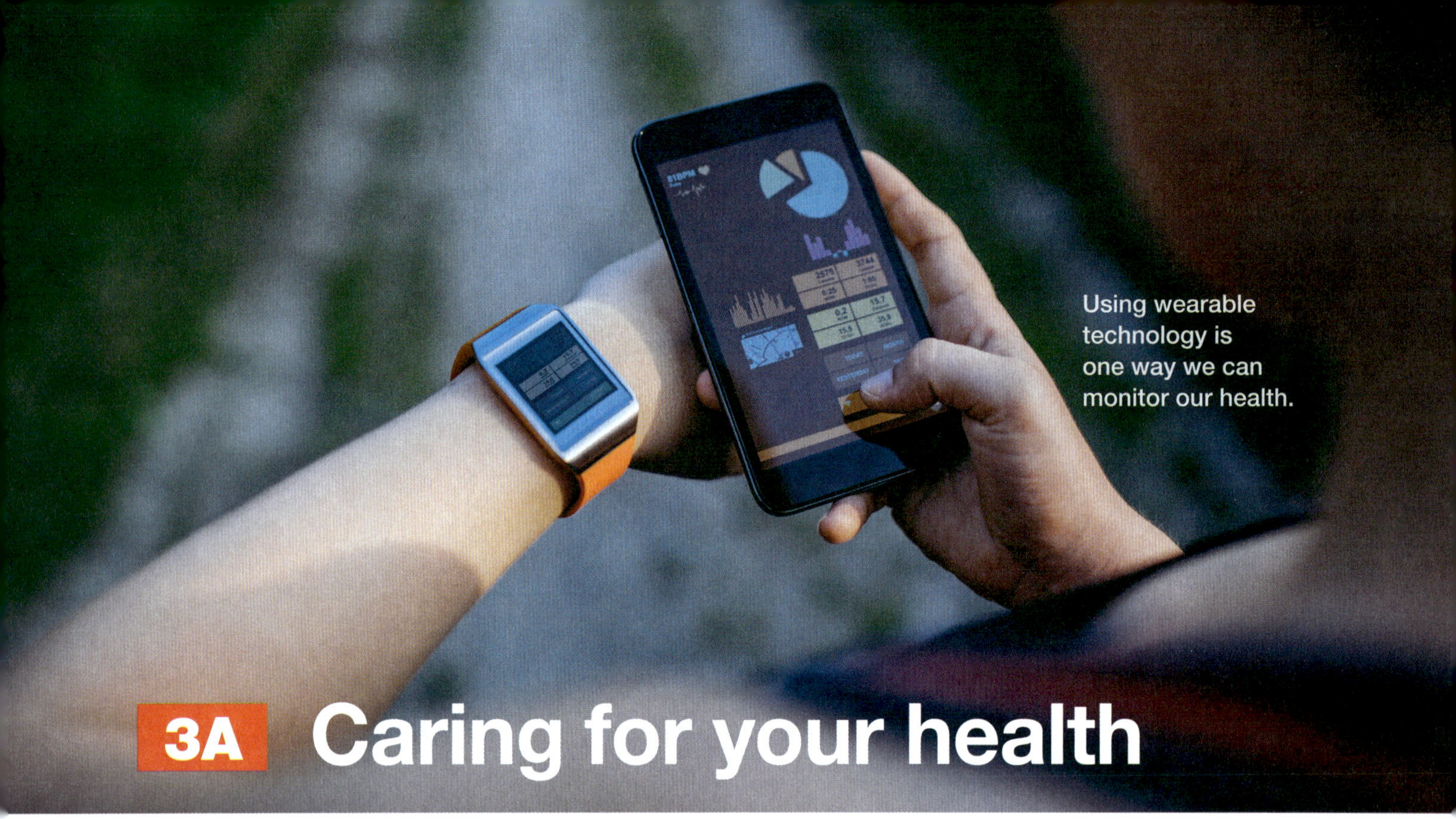

Using wearable technology is one way we can monitor our health.

3A Caring for your health

VOCABULARY Talking about healthcare

A ▶ **3.2** Complete the information using the words in the box. Two words are extra. Then listen and check your answers.

treatments	caregiver	elderly	suffer from
cure	monitor	wearable	motivate

As populations grow older and the number of [1]________ people rises, healthcare is becoming increasingly expensive and complicated. Elderly people naturally [2]________ more health problems and may need a variety of [3]________. One solution is [4]________ technology—small, light devices that people can carry with them. By measuring a person's heart rate, for example, these devices can [5]________ a person's health. This information can help the [6]________, nurse, or doctor take care of patients better.

B Complete the sentences. Circle the correct words.

1 The (**treatment** / **healthcare**) for a bad back involves lots of rest.

2 There is still no (**cure** / **caregiver**) for many types of cancer.

3 People who are overweight and don't exercise are likely to (**suffer from** / **cure**) health issues.

4 Many fitness (**treatments** / **wearables**) monitor things such as the number of steps people take.

5 Devices that track exercise can help (**monitor** / **motivate**) people to be more active.

C Work with a partner. Discuss these questions.

1 Does your country have a high percentage of elderly people?

2 Are there any special healthcare services for them?

LISTENING My health routine

Talking about the benefits of something

We can use expressions like the ones below to describe the benefits of something.

It's great for … *It works well for people who …* *I find … most useful.*

A ▶ 3.3 Watch Kate Chong talk about her health routine. Check (✓) the ways she stays healthy.

- ☐ by getting enough rest
- ☐ by having a balanced diet
- ☐ by cycling to work every day
- ☐ by exercising every weekend

Kate Chong leads an active lifestyle.

B ▶ 3.3 Watch again. Complete the sentences. Circle the correct words.

1 Chong uses a running app on her phone to keep track of (**the weather conditions on each run** / **how far she's run**).

2 She likes the app because it (**is easy to use** / **helps her stay disciplined**).

3 Chong's cycling app allows her to (**compare cycling data with friends** / **train with a virtual cycling partner**).

C **CRITICAL THINKING**

Reflecting Work with a partner. What other ways do you think technology can help improve people's health?

SPEAKING Talking about staying healthy

A ▶ 3.4 Is Speaker A motivated to keep fit?

A: You seem pretty fit. Do you do any regular exercise?

B: Yeah. I go to the gym a few times a week.

A: What do you do there?

B: I do some stretching and then usually run for half an hour or so.

A: Don't you get bored? How do you motivate yourself?

B: Well, I often go with a friend. Also, I recently bought a wearable. It helps me learn more about my lifestyle habits, and motivates me to do more. How about you? Do you do much exercise?

A: Not very often. I'm usually too tired after work. Maybe I should sign up for a class at the gym. I think that will make me more motivated!

B Practice the conversation with a partner.

C Work with a partner. Talk about what you do to keep fit, how you motivate yourself, and if you use any technology to keep track of your health. Use the expressions in blue above to help you.

Do you do any regular exercise?

I try to go swimming every week.

3B Tech in healthcare

LANGUAGE FOCUS Discussing mobile healthcare

A ▶ 3.5 Read the information. Do you look up health-related information online? What do you look for?

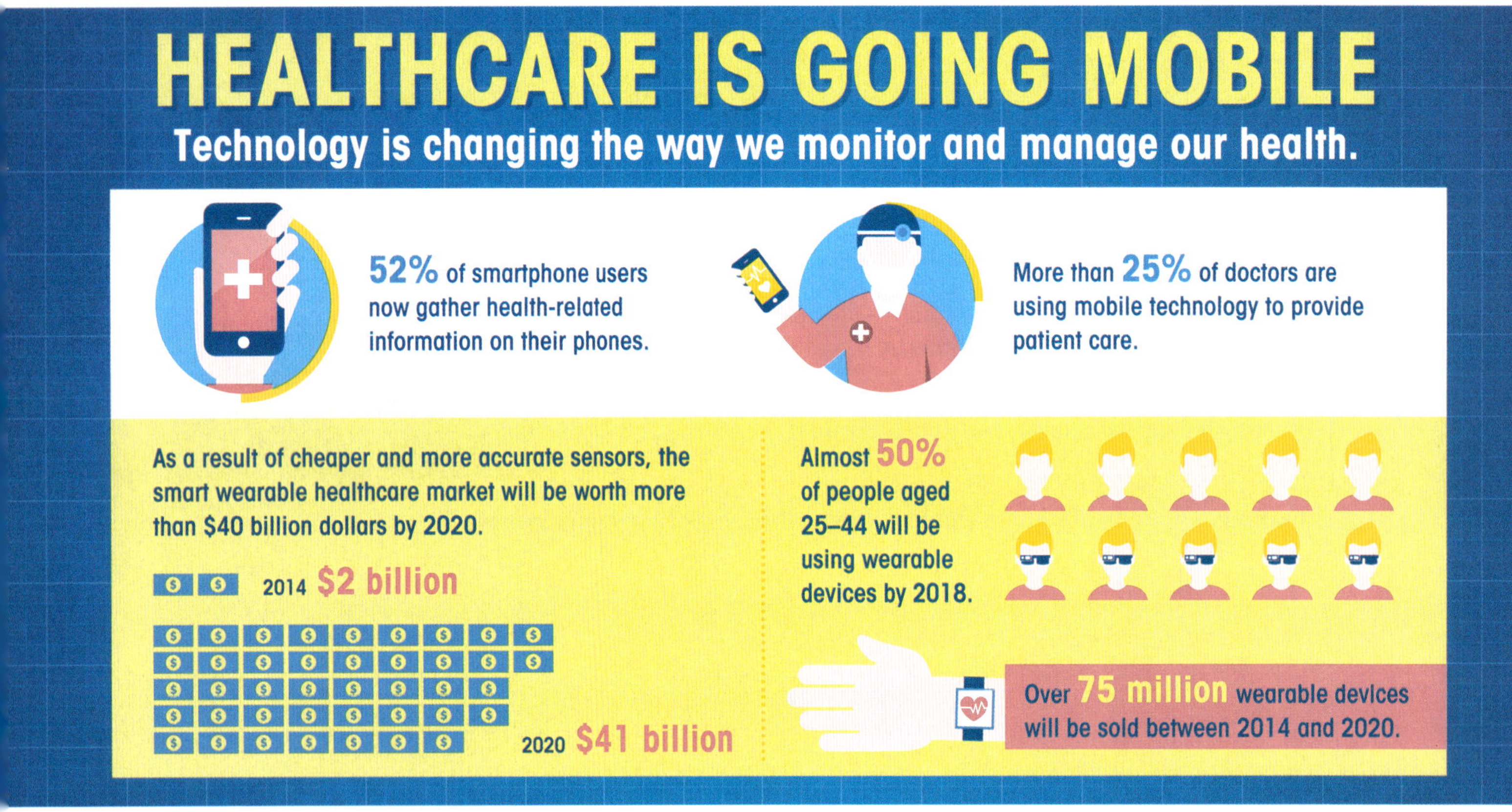

B ▶ 3.6 Listen to the conversation. What does the woman recommend her friend to do? Discuss with a partner.

C ▶ 3.7 Watch and study the language in the chart.

Talking about cause and effect

Obesity can lead to other health problems, so it's important to have a healthy diet.

Health apps are becoming popular nowadays because people are more concerned about their health.

Elderly people usually require more medical care due to age-related illnesses.

You should eat less red meat, as too much of it can lead to heart disease.

As a result of improvements in medical technology, we are able to treat more illnesses.

Gathering personal health information has become easier because of the Internet.

For more information on **cause and effect**, see Grammar Summary 3 on page 184.

D ▶ 3.6 Listen to the conversation in **B** again. Complete the sentences from the conversation.

1 "I had a terrible night's sleep ______________ I kept waking up."

2 "I can't really focus in class sometimes ______________ I'm so tired."

3 "You'll get to know your sleep habits, ______________ you can see what helps you sleep."

E Match the two parts of the sentences.

1 A lot of people are buying wearables ○	○ so they're easy to carry around.
2 Many lives are saved each year ○	○ people can find out a lot more about their health.
3 Fitness devices are usually small and light, ○	○ because of improvements in medical technology.
4 As a result of improvements in mobile healthcare, ○	○ because they are interested in monitoring their health.

F ▶ 3.8 Complete the information. Circle the correct words. Then listen and check your answers.

Michael Lwin is a Burmese-American who moved back to Myanmar in 2012. When Lwin met his cousin Yar Zar Minn Htoo in Myanmar, he found out that his cousin had gotten hepatitis B—a serious disease—[1](**so** / **because**) a rural doctor had used dirty needles and infected Yar Zar Minn Htoo with the virus.

Lwin and Yar Zar Minn Htoo wanted to improve people's access to healthcare in their country, [2](**so** / **as**) in 2012, they worked together to start Koe Koe Tech. They created Kyan Mar Yae—the country's first general health app—which sends personalized messages to users' phones. [3](**As** / **Because of**) more than 90 percent of the population in Myanmar use smartphones, this is an effective way to provide more people with access to healthcare information and advice. According to Lwin, this app will also benefit the women and children of Myanmar, [4](**due to** / **as**) 70 percent of births take place outside a hospital.

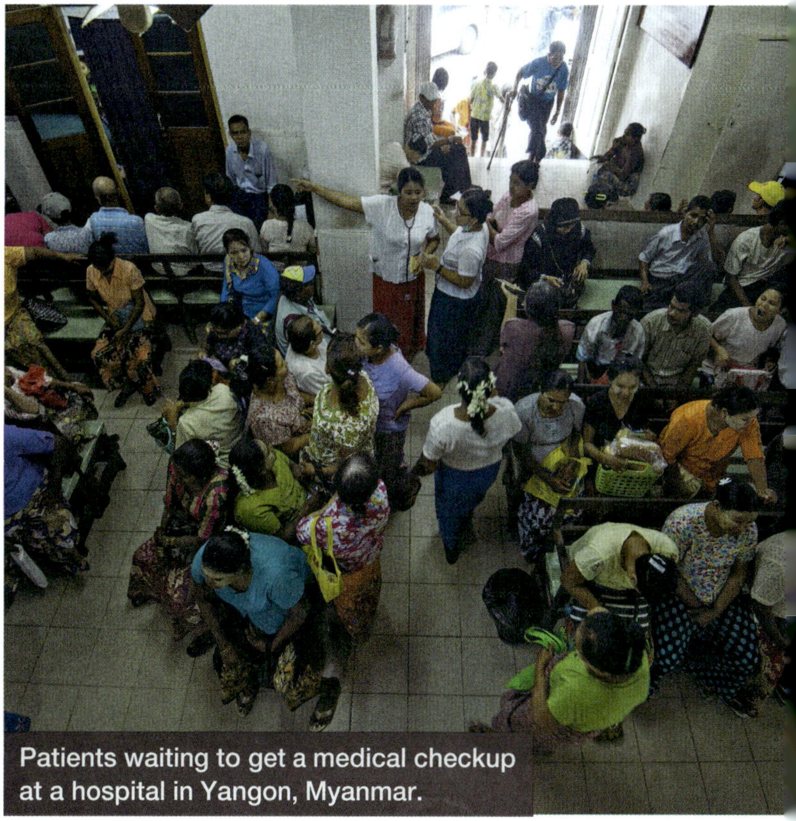

Patients waiting to get a medical checkup at a hospital in Yangon, Myanmar.

SPEAKING Talking about healthcare tech

Work with a partner. You are going to read about a type of healthcare technology that could be used in the future. **Student A:** Turn to page 165. **Student B:** Turn to page 166. Describe the technology you have read about to your partner, and explain the effects it could have on people in the future.

3C The challenge of Alzheimer's

PRE-READING Predicting

Skim the first paragraph. What kinds of challenges do you think there are in countries where people live longer?

▶ 3.9

For the first time in history, there are more people above the age of 65 than children below the age of five. As populations grow older, aging societies will begin to face major challenges—such as the provision of healthcare.

Elderly people have a higher chance of suffering from illnesses such as diabetes, cancer, and heart disease. Providing proper healthcare facilities and treatment is expensive, and the rising cost of healthcare puts a lot of **pressure** on the working population. In Europe, for example, there are currently four working people supporting one elderly person. By 2050, this number will fall to two workers per elderly person.

One common health problem that affects elderly people is Alzheimer's disease. Alzheimer's—the most common type of dementia—affects a person's memory, **behavior**, and thinking. Because of memory loss and behavioral changes, people with Alzheimer's may slowly become unable to take care of themselves, eventually requiring **constant** care from family members or caregivers.

There is no cure for Alzheimer's at the moment—drugs can only treat its symptoms.

Many developed countries are experiencing aging populations. One of the most notable examples is Japan. Japan's population is rapidly aging as a result of fewer babies being born and people living longer. By 2060, four in ten people will be over the age of 65.

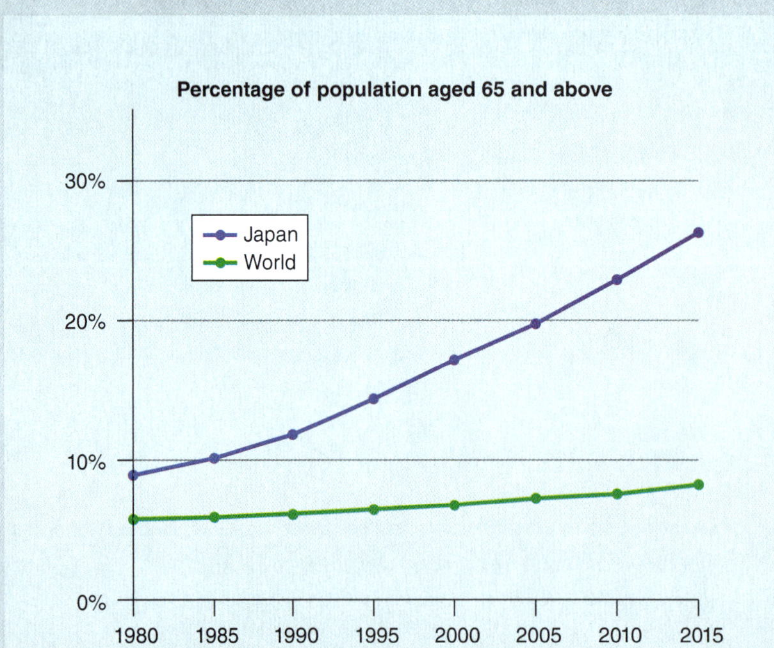

Source: UN Population Division

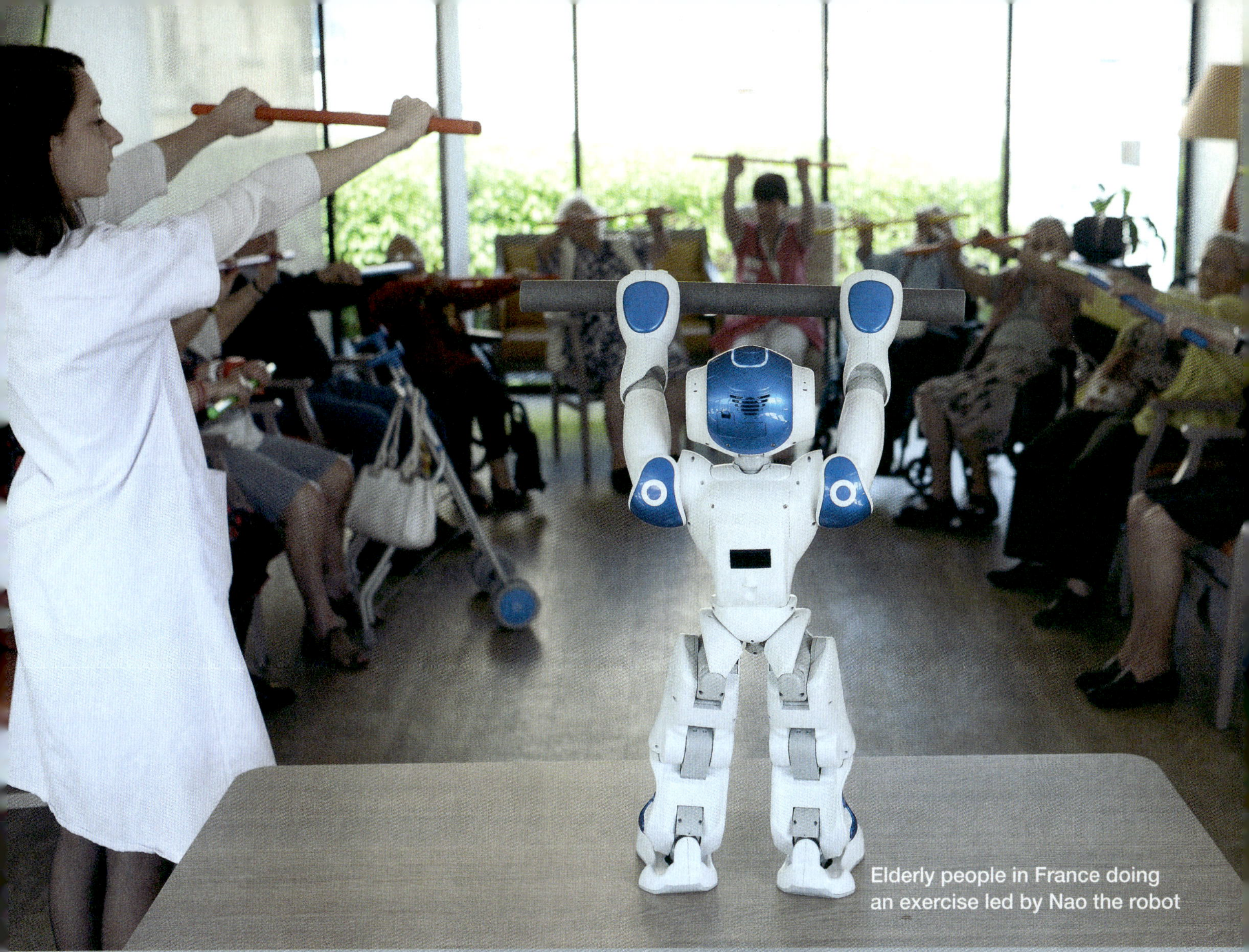

Elderly people in France doing an exercise led by Nao the robot

But technology can improve the lives of those living with the condition by making it easier for them to go about their daily activities. For example, tracking devices placed in watches or jewelry can monitor where a person is. Automated[1] reminders can also be stored in motion sensors and placed around the house. When a sensor detects movement, it can play a recorded voice message to remind the person to lock the door or turn off the stove.

Alzheimer's disease is a huge challenge, but we may be getting close to finding a solution. In the future, it might be possible to treat Alzheimer's without using drugs. A team of researchers in Australia has created a form of technology that can send sound waves into the brain. These sound waves help to clear waste in the brain that contributes to Alzheimer's. The team has tested their technology and found that it helped to restore[2] memory in 75 percent of mice. Work on the technology isn't complete, but, if successful, it could **prevent** memory loss in people with Alzheimer's. "I think this really does fundamentally change our understanding of how to treat this disease," says Professor Jürgen Götz, a co-author of the study, "and I foresee a great future for this **approach**."

[1] **automated:** *adj.* run by a machine or computer

[2] **restore:** *v.* to return something to its original state

UNDERSTANDING MAIN IDEAS

What is the main idea of the passage?

a There is a need to better understand the cause of Alzheimer's disease.

b Technology may be able to help tackle some of the problems of people with Alzheimer's.

c Many elderly people are unable to afford the cost of treating Alzheimer's.

UNDERSTANDING CAUSE AND EFFECT

Complete the diagram showing causes and effects.

CAUSE	→	EFFECT
Cost of healthcare [1] ____________ due to the need for medical facilities and treatment for the elderly population.	→	There is huge pressure on the [2] ____________ population to support the cost of healthcare.
People with Alzheimer's may experience memory [3] ____________ and behavioral [4] ____________.	→	They require [5] ____________ care from their family or caregivers.

UNDERSTANDING DETAILS

Choose the correct option to complete each sentence.

1 Alzheimer's is a disease that mainly affects the ______.

a muscles **b** blood **c** brain

2 Australian researchers have shown that it may be possible to ______ people with Alzheimer's.

a prevent memory loss in **b** increase the sleep quality of **c** improve the communication ability of

BUILDING VOCABULARY

A Complete the sentences using the words in blue from the passage.

1 Researchers are still finding ways to ____________ people from getting cancer.

2 Family members are often under a lot of ____________ caring for people with Alzheimer's.

3 A ____________ decrease in the birth rate can cause populations to shrink.

4 When an idea doesn't work well, you should try a different ____________.

5 Scientists sometimes study the ____________ of animals to find out what we can learn from them.

B **CRITICAL THINKING**

Inferring What is the author's attitude toward finding solutions to the challenges of Alzheimer's? What evidence is there from the article?

3D My simple invention, designed to keep my grandfather safe

TEDTALKS

KENNETH SHINOZUKA has been designing smart products since he was six years old. Ever since his grandfather was **diagnosed** with Alzheimer's disease, Kenneth's family has **struggled** to care for him. **Concerned** by this, Kenneth designed a smart device. The **sensor** in the device **detects** pressure when someone steps on it.

Kenneth Shinozuka's idea worth spreading is that smart uses of sensory technology can improve our lives as we age—particularly for Alzheimer's patients and those who care for them.

PREVIEWING

Read the paragraphs above. Match each **bold** word to its meaning. You will hear these words in the TED Talk.

1 worried ______
2 notices something ______
3 had difficulty ______
4 identified a medical condition ______
5 a device that responds to things like light or sound ______

VIEWING

A ▶ 3.10 Watch Part 1 of the TED Talk. Choose the correct options.

1 Kenneth's grandfather's condition brought a lot of stress to his family because he often ______.
  - **a** couldn't go to sleep
  - **b** wandered off by himself
  - **c** couldn't express his thoughts

2 Kenneth was worried about his aunt's well-being because she was ______.
  - **a** not eating healthy meals
  - **b** often getting sick
  - **c** not getting enough rest at night

B ▶ **3.11** Watch Part 2 of the TED Talk. Complete the labels describing how Kenneth Shinozuka's invention works. Then number the steps from 1–4.

1 Patient puts sock on.

2 When the patient ____________ on the floor, the pressure sensor detects a(n) ____________ in pressure.

3 Sensor sends a wireless alert to the caregiver's ____________.

4 Smartphone makes a(n) ____________.

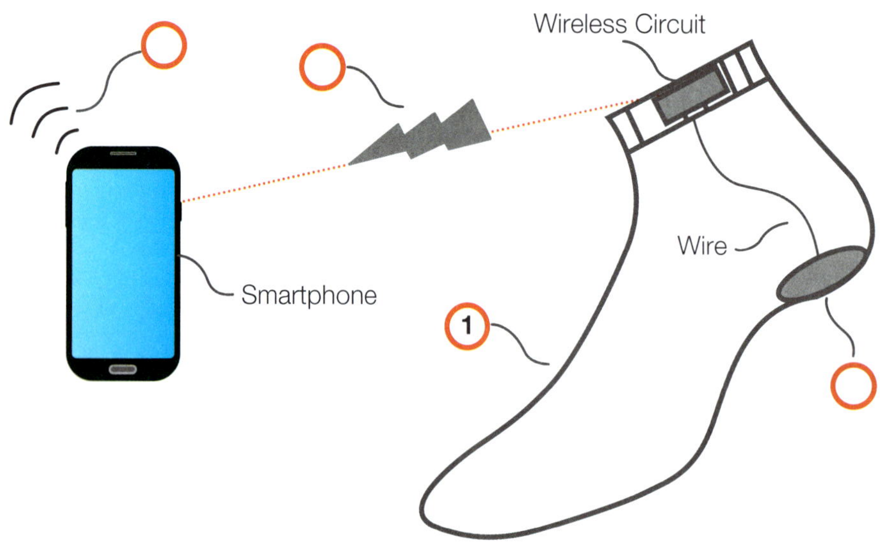

C ▶ **3.12** Watch Part 3 of the TED Talk. Complete the diagram showing Kenneth Shinozuka's invention and research process.

Invented a smart sock → Tested it on his [1] ____________ → Carried out tests at residential [2] ____________ ____________ in California → Gathered [3] ____________, e.g., some people don't want to [4] ____________ to sleep at night → Improved device

D CRITICAL THINKING

Inferring Work with a partner. Look at the quote below. What other correlations would you look for?

"I'm currently examining correlations between the frequency of a patient's nightly wandering and his or her daily activities and diet."

VOCABULARY IN CONTEXT

A ▶ **3.13** Watch the excerpts from the TED Talk. Choose the correct meaning of the words.

B Complete the sentences with the words from the box.

firsthand	stem from	incorporate	keep an eye on	overwhelming

1 Caregivers or family members need to ______________ people with Alzheimer's.

2 Some medical conditions such as obesity may ______________ bad lifestyle choices.

3 There is ______________ evidence that smoking causes lung cancer.

4 Inventors have to ______________ feedback from users to improve their creations.

5 Many caregivers experience ______________ how hard it is for people with Alzheimer's to get on with daily life.

PRESENTATION SKILLS Opening with interesting facts

Start your presentation with interesting facts to get your audience's attention.

Did you know that ...?

You may not know that ...

Here is a fact you may not know ...

What do you think ...?

▶ **3.14** Watch part of Kenneth Shinozuka's TED Talk. Complete the facts he gives.

1 "What's the ______________ threat to Americans' health? Cancer? Heart attacks? Diabetes? The answer is actually none of these; it's Alzheimer's disease."

2 "Every ______________, someone in the United States is diagnosed with Alzheimer's."

3 "As the number of Alzheimer's patients ______________ by the year 2050, caring for them, as well as the rest of the aging population, will become an overwhelming societal challenge."

Kenneth Shinozuka hopes to turn his invention into a product that can help people with Alzheimer's.

3E Healthcare solutions

COMMUNICATE Innovative healthcare solutions

A Work in small groups. Choose one of the scenarios below.

Scenario A
Person A is 70 years old. He is no longer able to walk more than a few meters on his own. He lives alone and is finding basic chores like cleaning and shopping very difficult.

Scenario B
Person B is 65 years old. She needs to take medicine regularly as she suffers from several medical conditions. However, she often forgets to take the medicine. Sometimes she even takes the wrong medicine or the wrong amount.

Scenario C
Person C is a 24-year-old athlete. He is training for a competition next month. He has to keep to a strict, healthy diet in order to be at his best during the competition. However, his training schedules are very busy and he doesn't have enough time to plan his meals properly.

B In your group, brainstorm possible tech solutions that could help make life easier for the person. Think about the problem the person faces, how it affects his or her daily life, and how technology can help.

C Take turns explaining your group's scenario and presenting your tech solution to the class. Then vote for the most innovative idea.

Talking about problems and solutions

He finds it difficult to …	*This … can aid the person in …*
He struggles with …	*One way to improve the situation is …*

The person in our scenario faces the problem of …

He can use this tech product to help with …

WRITING Expressing an opinion

Write a short letter to a company that develops tech products for healthcare purposes. Explain the healthcare issue you discussed above, giving your opinion on the best actions to help with similar cases.

Elderly people who live alone may need some help in their daily lives. A possible way to help them is …

Tech products such as this software for medical students can help improve the quality of healthcare.

Presentation 1

MODEL PRESENTATION

A Complete the transcript of the presentation using the words in the box.

finished	because	going to tell	will make
did you know	so	spent	ends up

Hi. I'm Lori. It's nice to be here today. [1]________________ that in the Pacific Ocean, there's a huge body of plastic trash floating around that's twice the size of Texas? We have a really big problem with trash in the world. Today, I'm [2]________________ you about what I do to help and how you can get involved, too.

A lot of trash [3]________________ on the beach, in rivers, or in the sea. All this trash harms humans and wildlife [4]________________ it pollutes our environment and poisons our food sources. I live near the sea, [5]________________ I decided to volunteer for a beach clean-up a few Sundays ago. There were about 20 of us. We had our own buckets and gloves, and [6]________________ a couple of hours picking up all the trash. Here's a picture of the trash we collected. And this picture shows how the beach looked when we [7]________________. Seeing the clean beach at the end was really satisfying. It was fun, too, and I made some new friends.

So, that's how I help. I can only play a small role, of course, but when lots of people join in, it makes a big difference. I encourage you to try a clean-up. It's fun, easy to do, and worthwhile. And you [8]________________ new friends, too. Thanks for listening.

B ▶ **P.1** Watch the presentation and check your answers.

C ▶ **P.1** Review the list of presentation skills from Units 1–3 below. Which does the speaker use? Check (✓) them as you watch again. Then compare with a partner.

The speaker …

- helps the audience visualize by
  - doing a demonstration ☐
  - giving interesting facts ☐
  - telling a story ☐
  - using visuals ☐
- comments on visuals ☐
- opens with an interesting fact ☐

D ▶ **P.1** Do you remember the way Lori draws attention to the visuals? Complete the sentences below. Then watch and check. Notice her gestures.

"________________ of the trash we collected. And ________________ how the beach looked when we finished."

YOUR TURN

A You are going to plan and give a short presentation about how you can make a difference. Think about what you want to do, and make notes in the box below.

How I can make a difference

Why I think it can help

B Look at the useful phrases in the box below. Think about which ones you will need in your presentation.

Useful phrases

Beginning:	*It's great to be here today.* *Did you know that ...?* *I'm going to ... / I'd like to ...*
Commenting on visuals:	*This picture shows ...* *Here's a picture of ...*
Concluding:	*So, in conclusion, ...* *I encourage you to ...* *Thanks for listening.*

C Work with a partner. Take turns giving your presentation using your notes. Use some of the presentation skills from Units 1–3. As you listen, check (✓) each skill your partner uses.

The speaker ...

- helps the audience visualize by
  - doing a demonstration ☐
  - giving interesting facts ☐
  - telling a story ☐
  - using visuals ☐
- comments on visuals ☐
- opens with an interesting fact ☐

D Give your partner some feedback on their talk. Include at least two things you liked and one thing that could be improved.

That was a great presentation. You gave interesting facts and included beautiful pictures. Maybe you could talk a bit more about the pictures.

4 Designing the Web

“Consider the fact that Google processes over one billion search queries every day, that every minute, over 100 hours of footage are uploaded to YouTube.”

Margaret Gould Stewart
User experience designer, TED speaker

UNIT GOALS

In this unit, you will ...

- talk about digital products and how they are designed.
- read about designing websites for millions of people.
- watch a TED Talk about designing for all kinds of users.

WARM UP

▶ **4.1** Watch part of Margaret Gould Stewart's TED Talk. Answer the questions with a partner.

1 What examples of classic design can you think of?

2 What do you think Stewart means by designs that "live inside your pocket"?

4A Technology and design

VOCABULARY Describing website features

A 4.2 Complete the labels using the words in the box. Then listen and check your answers.

search	browse	review	download
rate	button	log in	logo

This is the website's [1] ______________ .

Use the [2] ______________ box to look for posts you're interested in.

Enter your user name and password to [3] ______________ .

You can [4] ______________ the sidebar for the latest posts.

Click to read the [8] ______________ of a café.

Click on the "share" [5] ______________ to send the link to someone else.

You can [6] ______________ the recipe by clicking on this icon.

Click on one of these icons to [7] ______________ the post.

B Complete the sentences. Circle the correct words.

1. McDonald's golden arches and Starbucks's mermaid are examples of famous (**logos** / **buttons**).
2. A lot of people go online to write (**downloads** / **reviews**) of the products they buy.
3. Customers usually (**rate** / **log in**) a product based on price and how user-friendly it is.
4. It's easy to look for information by (**downloading** / **browsing**) the Web.

C Work with a partner. What kinds of apps do you usually download? Have you ever written an online review?

I usually download news apps. I like to keep up with current events.

I prefer downloading gaming apps. My favorite is ...

LISTENING Designing websites

Stating your points
Here are some commonly used phrases for listing points.
First/Second, ... *Also, ...* *One other thing is ...*

A ▶ 4.3 Watch web designer Carrie Cousins talk about the work she does. How does she define "user experience"? Discuss with a partner.

Carrie Cousins has more than 15 years of experience in the media industry.

B ▶ 4.4 Watch Cousins talk about the things she focuses on when designing a website. Match them to their explanations.

1 functionality ○	○ The content is nice to look at.
2 readability ○	○ The website solves a user problem.
3 usability ○	○ The website is easy to navigate.

C **CRITICAL THINKING**

Evaluating Work with a partner. What other things do you think are important to consider when designing a website? Why?

SPEAKING Talking about making decisions

A ▶ 4.5 How did Speaker B decide what product to buy?

A: Hey, is that a new tablet? I didn't know you had one.

B: Yeah, I looked around and finally decided on this one.

A: It looks great. How did you decide which one to get?

B: Well, I checked out the company's website and watched their promotional videos. I also read a lot of reviews online.

A: Did you compare prices?

B: Yeah, this model is the best, I think. It's not the most expensive, and it has pretty good features for the price.

A: What do you like most about it?

B: The size. It's smaller than standard tablets, so I can easily carry it around.

B Practice the conversation with a partner.

C Work with a partner. Think of something you bought recently and describe your experience. Use the expressions in blue above to help you.

I bought a new pair of earphones over the weekend.

How did you decide which ones to get?

I looked around online and then ...

4B User experience

LANGUAGE FOCUS Discussing the influence of user reviews

A ▶ 4.6 Read the information. How often do you buy something online? How important are user reviews to you?

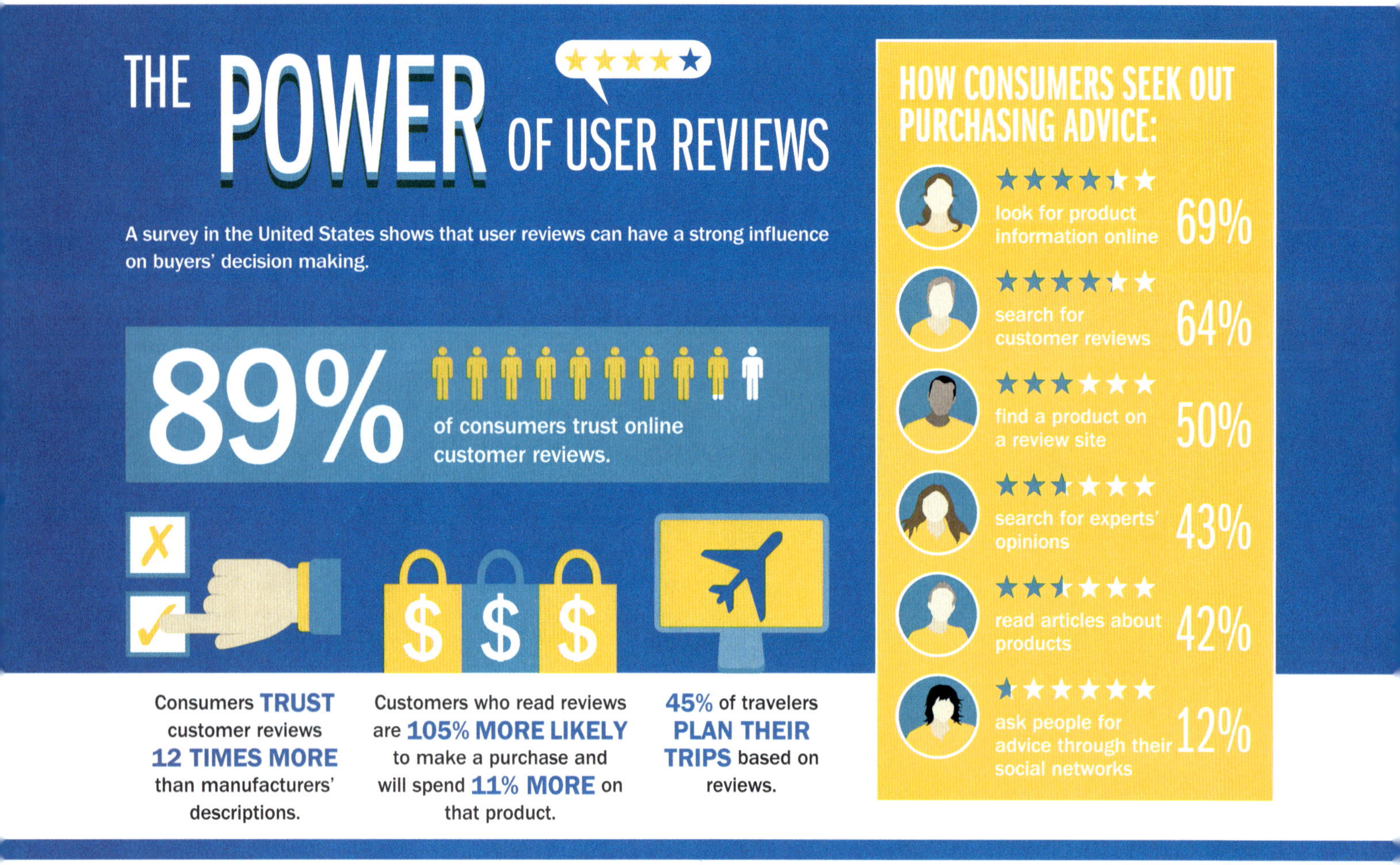

B ▶ 4.7 Listen to the conversation. What do the speakers decide to do? Discuss with a partner.

C ▶ 4.8 Watch and study the language in the chart.

Comparing products and services

I think using a navigation app is easier than looking at a printed map.

I think it's much more efficient to work on a desktop than on a tablet computer.

Many consumers search online for the best product available before buying.

Some smartphones are just as expensive as laptops these days.

These days, people use their phones in very different ways from just ten years ago.

Smartphones today have pretty much the same functions as computers.

For more information on **making comparisons**, see Grammar Summary 4 on pages 184–185.

D ▶ **4.7** Listen to the conversation in B again. Circle the correct words.

1 The woman is (**as confident as** / **more confident than**) the man about the reliability of online reviews.

2 The man thinks that checking out the restaurant in person is (**better than** / **not as good as**) reading online reviews.

E Complete the sentences to make comparisons. Add suitable comparison words as necessary.

1 Sometimes, cheaper products may be just ______________ (reliable) more expensive products—the price may not mean a difference in quality.

2 One of the ______________ (important) things in website design is making it easy for users to find information.

3 Online prices are usually ______________ (not, expensive) store prices.

4 I bought a shirt online, but when it arrived, it was ______________ (different) how it looked in the pictures.

5 Some people think shopping at an actual store is ______________ (good) buying things online because they can touch and try out the products.

F ▶ **4.9** Complete the information. Circle the correct words. Then listen and check your answers.

It has become a lot [1](**more** / **better**) common for consumers to look for reviews online when making decisions on what to buy. It helps them find out what other people think of a restaurant or an item they have bought. According to a survey, consumers think that customer reviews are 12 times [2](**more trustworthy than** / **most trustworthy**) the manufacturer's product description. The growing influence of online reviews means that businesses have to work hard to provide the [3](**better** / **best**) products to stay competitive. Online comparison sites also make it [4](**as easy as** / **easier than**) before for consumers to compare prices. They can quickly find out if a business is charging them [5](**as different as** / **the same as**) others for a product or service.

The Yelp app allows users to read reviews of different businesses.

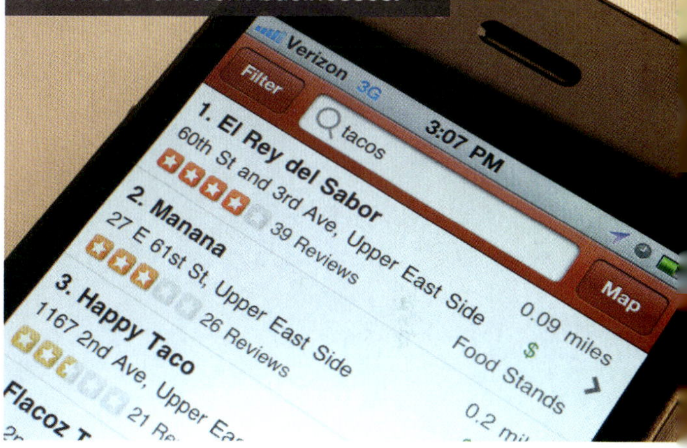

SPEAKING Making decisions based on user reviews

A Work with a partner. You are planning to buy a virtual reality headset. Turn to page 168 and read the reviews of two products. Discuss the following questions.

1 What features do you think are most important?

2 How do the products compare in terms of the features you're looking for?

B Decide which product you would buy. Describe the product you chose and give reasons for your choice.

I chose number 1. It's lighter and cheaper, so …

Having a lot of features is good, but the price …

4C Website design on a giant scale

PRE-READING Skimming

Skim the article. The purpose of the article is to ______.

a explain how difficult it is to design huge websites

b discuss some lessons in huge website design

c explore the common challenges of digital design

4.10

Margaret Gould Stewart has designed for some of the giants of the Internet, including Google, YouTube, and Facebook. Here are two lessons she has learned from her experience designing for Internet users.

LOOK BEYOND DATA

For a long time, Facebook had a tool that allowed people to report photos as **spam** or abuse.[1] But of the cases reported, only a small percentage of the photos were actually offensive.[2] One of the designers on the team felt there probably was a reason for this, so he studied the cases carefully. He found that in most cases users just didn't like the photos of themselves their friends had posted, and wanted them taken down. To enable people to report cases like these, the Facebook team added a new feature. This feature allowed people to message their friends to ask them to take the photo down. But only 20 percent of people used the function.

The team worked on the case further—it spoke to communications experts and studied rules of polite language. It discovered that users didn't just want to tell their friends to take the photo down—they wanted to tell their friends how the photo made them feel. So the team made a small change. People could select a message to explain why they didn't like it, such as, "It's embarrassing." This small change had a huge **impact**—60 percent of people who reported photos used the function. Surveys showed that people on both sides of the conversation felt better as a result.

While data about how people are using a product can help designers make decisions, it isn't always as simple as following the numbers. Other factors such as intuition,[3] research, and testing of design are equally important. As Stewart points out, "Data can help you make a good design great, but it will never make a bad design good."

Mark Zuckerberg, CEO of Facebook, introducing the new features of its messaging app

INTRODUCE CHANGE CAREFULLY

At one time, YouTube was looking for ways to **encourage** more people to rate videos. When Stewart and her team looked into the data, they found that most people were only using either the highest rating (five stars) or the lowest rating (one star). Almost no one was using two, three, or four stars. So the team decided to simplify the rating—it gave users a choice between good or bad: thumbs up or thumbs down.

YouTube tried to prepare people for this change by sharing data about how the five-star rating system wasn't being used as intended. It announced that it was going to change the system to match user behavior. When the change was made, it was still **frustrating** for some users as they had become **attached** to the old design. However, because of the preparatory steps taken earlier, it was easier for YouTube to get users to accept the change.

This experience shows that even when huge websites try to manage change carefully, it's impossible to completely avoid negative responses. Any changes—even small improvements—need to be introduced carefully.

[1] **abuse:** *n.* improper use of something
[2] **offensive:** *adj.* making someone feel hurt or uncomfortable
[3] **intuition:** *n.* a natural feeling about something

SUMMARIZING KEY POINTS

Complete the diagram summarizing Margaret Gould Stewart's experiences.

Lessons from Stewart's experiences

Facebook

Situation

People used a tool for reporting spam to report photos of [1] ________________ that they didn't like.

What Facebook did

Facebook added a feature that allowed people to [2] ________________ their friend to take down the photo and explain how the photo made them feel.

Lesson

Data is important in helping designers [3] ________________, but it must be looked at carefully.

YouTube

Situation

People only used [4] ________________ and [5] ________________ ratings on a five-star rating system.

What YouTube did

YouTube shared [6] ________________ about how people were using its rating system before simplifying it to either thumbs [7] ________________ or thumbs [8] ________________.

Lesson

It's important to manage [9] ________________ carefully.

BUILDING VOCABULARY

A Match the words in blue from the passage to their definitions.

1 spam	an effect
2 impact	having a strong liking for something
3 encourage	unwanted emails
4 frustrating	annoying, irritating
5 attached	to make someone more likely to do something

B Complete the sentences using the words in A.

1 I get more ________________ than regular emails.

2 YouTube made its rating system simpler to ________________ more people to rate videos.

3 Creative innovations can have a big ________________ on how people interact with one another.

4 Some people may find learning how to use a new cell phone a(n) ________________ experience.

5 Many people become emotionally ________________ to their smartphones.

C CRITICAL THINKING

Inferring Why do you think more people sent a message to their friend after Facebook allowed them to explain how the photo made them feel? Discuss with a partner.

4D How giant websites design for you (and a billion others, too)

TEDTALKS

MARGARET GOULD STEWART has spent her career asking the question, "How do we design user experiences that change the world?" She has managed user experiences for some of the most visited websites in the world, including YouTube and Facebook. The wide reach of these websites means that Stewart has had to deal with **unprecedented** challenges and **constraints**.

Margaret Gould Stewart's idea worth spreading is that designing at a global **scale** requires both the **audacity** to believe your product is needed by the whole world, and the **humility** to understand that your audience is far more important than you as a designer.

PREVIEWING

Read the paragraphs above. Match each **bold** word to its meaning. You will hear these words in the TED Talk.

1 the quality of not being proud ________________

2 confidence or courage to take risks ________________

3 the size or level of something ________________

4 things that limit what you can do ________________

5 not done before or hasn't happened in the past ________________

VIEWING

A ▶ 4.11 Watch Part 1 of the TED Talk. Check (✓) the sentences about design challenges that Margaret Gould Stewart mentions.

☐ Designers need to believe that their products are something the world wants.

☐ Users differ greatly in the kinds of things they want.

☐ Designers must understand that their work may have an important impact on people's lives.

☐ There are no fixed ways of doing things or guaranteed success when designing at scale.

B ▶ 4.12 Watch Part 2 of the TED Talk. Which of the following describes the lesson learned from designing the Facebook "Like" button?

a When you are designing on a huge scale, every detail—no matter how small it seems—is important.

b It's necessary to spend a lot of time and effort redesigning elements many times in order to make sure that the overall design fits the brand image.

c The smallest design details are the most important when designing on a huge scale, and you need to get the best designers to work on them.

C ▶ 4.13 Watch Part 3 of the TED Talk. Check (✓) the information Margaret Gould Stewart is likely to agree with.

People who design at scale ______.

- ☐ need to design for low-end cell phones
- ☐ should try using their products in different languages
- ☐ need to try out their products on both old and new phones
- ☐ should find ways to cut costs

D **CRITICAL THINKING**

Inferring Margaret Gould Stewart describes her work as something that isn't always glamorous. What does this say about the work she does?

" If you want to design for the whole world, you have to design for where people are, and not where you are. "

TEDTALKS

VOCABULARY IN CONTEXT

A ▶ **4.14** Watch the excerpts from the TED Talk. Choose the correct meaning of the words.

B Complete the sentences. Circle the correct words.

1. Designers can (**get their heads around** / **keep in touch with**) clients via email or social media.
2. Great designs are (**timeless** / **out of sync**)—they last forever.
3. Designers for huge websites should always (**keep in mind** / **get their heads around**) that change needs to be managed carefully.
4. It can be difficult to (**get your head around** / **keep in mind**) complicated computer terms unless they're explained simply.
5. I haven't done any design work in a while. I think I'm (**out of sync** / **keeping in touch**) with the latest trends in design.

PRESENTATION SKILLS Asking the audience questions

> Ask your audience questions to keep them engaged and to encourage them to think about the topic. Questions sometimes begin with *So* or *Now*.

A ▶ **4.15** Watch part of Margaret Gould Stewart's TED Talk. Complete the questions she uses in her talk.

1. "What do you think of when ____________________?"
2. "Now, why would we spend so much time on ____________________?"
3. "So how do we keep this ____________________?"
4. "So what does it mean to ____________________?"

B Work with a partner. Take turns explaining the steps for doing something. Practice using questions in your explanation.

Do you often receive spam? Here's how you can prevent ...

4E Making suggestions

COMMUNICATE Improving user experiences

A Work in groups. Think of a website you've used that could be better designed. Brainstorm ways to improve the design to create a better user experience. Consider the following questions.

What's good about the website? ____________________

____

What doesn't work so well? Why? ____________________

____

How can it be redesigned to make it better for people to use? ____________________

____

B Describe the website your group chose to the class and suggest ways it can be improved.

Describing user experience

The website is not very user-friendly … *It's easy/difficult to navigate …*
It has a simple/complicated design … *The organization of the website is confusing …*

The website has a cool design, but it's difficult to find …

Having fewer icons on the page would make the website …

WRITING Writing a review

Write a short review of your cell phone. Describe what you like and don't like about it, and suggest how it can be improved.

My cell phone is slim and light, but the screen is small. It's difficult to read the text when I'm typing because the keyboard is almost half the size of the screen. I would suggest …

Visitors testing the products on display at the Mobile World Congress in Barcelona

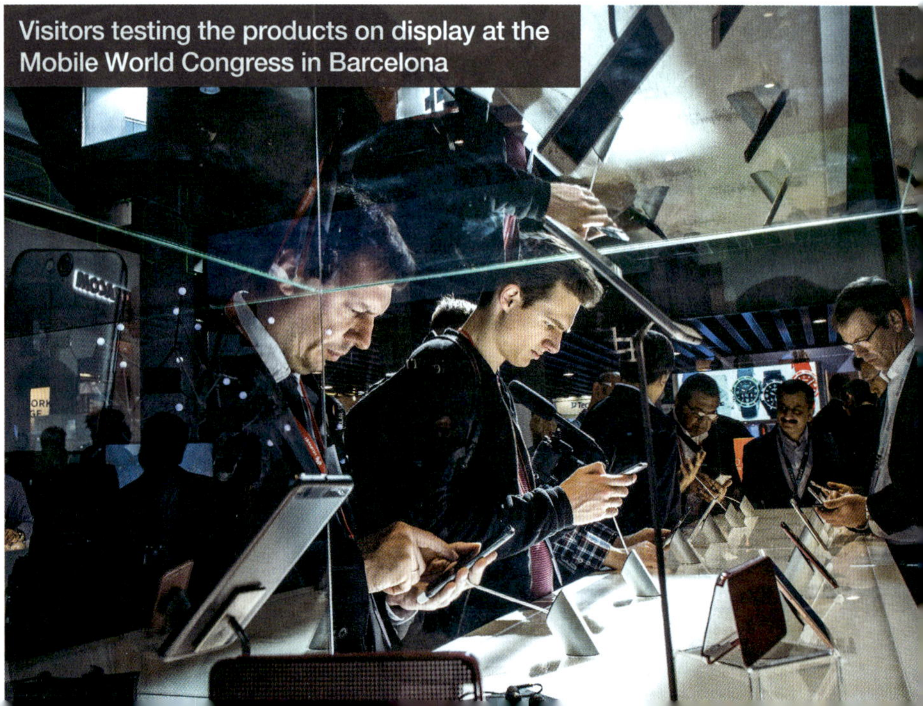

5 Community Builders

“... news from Vila Cruzeiro often is not good news. But Vila Cruzeiro is also the place where our story begins.”

Dre Urhahn and Jeroen Koolhaas
Artists, TED speakers

UNIT GOALS

In this unit, you will ...

- talk about communities and ways to improve them.
- read about a unique way a college is educating communities.
- watch a TED Talk about how people can work together to transform their communities.

WARM UP

▶ 5.1 Watch part of Koolhaas and Urhahn’s TED Talk. Answer the questions with a partner.

1 What do you know about Rio de Janeiro?

2 What do you think Vila Cruzeiro is like?

Volunteers and students painting a mural at a middle school in New York

5A Community building

VOCABULARY Making communities better

A Read the paragraph below. Then match each **bold** word to its definition.

Social **entrepreneurs** work to improve the lives of people and the **communities** they live in. Their businesses often focus on helping **underprivileged** people and communities. Sometimes, this involves **enhancing** or building **facilities** in the neighborhood, such as parks or schools. By creating jobs and improving environments, social entrepreneurs **empower** the underprivileged to make positive changes to their lives.

1 entrepreneurs ○	○ make someone stronger or more confident
2 communities ○	○ making something better
3 underprivileged ○	○ groups of people living together in an area
4 enhancing ○	○ places or services provided for a particular purpose
5 facilities ○	○ people who start businesses
6 empower ○	○ without the opportunities of the average person

B Complete the sentences. Circle the correct words.

1. Elon Musk is a very successful (**community** / **entrepreneur**) who has started businesses in travel and space technology.
2. Medical (**facilities** / **entrepreneurs**) like hospices and hospitals are needed to support the elderly population.
3. A strong and stable economy can (**enhance** / **empower**) the quality of life for the average person.
4. Mother Teresa dedicated her life to helping the (**empowered** / **underprivileged**) in India.

C Work with a partner. What does your city or community do to help the underprivileged?

LISTENING Creating green spaces

Listening for intonation

Intonation helps you differentiate between questions and statements. Questions often end with a high intonation, while statements often end with a low intonation.

A ▶ 5.2 Watch social entrepreneur Martín Andrade talk about his foundation, Mi Parque. What is the aim of the foundation?

a to reduce poverty and unemployment in Chile

b to create more green parks for the underprivileged in Chile

B ▶ 5.3 Watch and check (✓) the things that the foundation does.

☐ It improves the housing conditions of low-income families.

☐ It educates the public about the importance of green spaces.

☐ It gets locals directly involved in planning and carrying out projects.

☐ It works with the government to get funding.

Martín Andrade with some local children in Chile

C **CRITICAL THINKING**

Evaluating In what ways does having green spaces benefit the people of an urban community? Discuss with a partner.

SPEAKING Talking about my community

A ▶ 5.4 What does Speaker B think her community needs?

A: Hey, I heard you just moved to a new neighborhood. How do you like it so far?

B: On the whole, I really like it. It's peaceful and there's a real sense of community. For example, there are often local events like weekend markets.

A: What about the local facilities? Are there many?

B: There are a few local shops and a supermarket.

A: Hmm. It sounds like a pretty nice area to live.

B: Yeah. I think it could certainly benefit from a sports complex, though. Right now, there's nowhere to play sports.

A: Well, where I live in the city is *too* noisy. And there are hardly any green spaces! We could really do with a park.

B Practice the conversation with a partner.

C Tell a partner about your community, and what you like or dislike about it. Use the expressions in blue above to help you.

My community is really peaceful and quiet. I really like …

I think my community could benefit from a movie theater. A lot of people in my neighborhood …

5B Changing places

LANGUAGE FOCUS Beautifying public spaces

A 5.5 Read the information. Do you know any places that have been transformed?

THE TRANSFORMATION OF MALACCA RIVER

SINCE 2002, THE MALACCA RIVER IN MALAYSIA HAS GONE THROUGH A HUGE TRANSFORMATION.

WHAT WAS DONE

- **Pollution** was removed from the river.
- The riverbank was strengthened with **concrete walls**.
- A **barrier** was constructed to prevent flooding.
- 8 km of **walkways** were constructed on each side of the river.
- Riverside buildings were **repainted** with colorful murals.

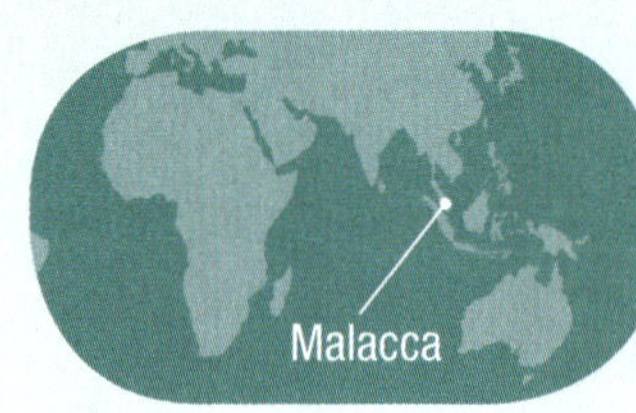

B 5.6 Listen to the conversation. What impression does the woman have of Malacca? Discuss with a partner.

C 5.7 Watch and study the language in the chart.

Talking about how places have changed

A construction company cleaned up the Malacca River. Architects transformed a church in Germany into a kindergarten.	The Malacca River was cleaned up. A church in Germany was transformed into a kindergarten.
A landscape architecture company designed the High Line Park in New York City. The Hong Kong government converted a landfill into a park.	The High Line Park in New York City was designed by a landscape architecture company. A landfill was converted into a park by the Hong Kong government.

For more information on **the passive**, see Grammar Summary 5 on page 185.

D ▶ **5.6** Listen to the conversation in **B** again. Complete the sentences from the conversation.

1 "But you wouldn't recognize it now. It's ______________________________."

2 "It's all ______________________________. All the old buildings ______________________________ into cool little shops and restaurants."

3 "And the buildings are brightly painted with murals that show Malacca's history and culture. They can ______________________________ all along the river."

E Complete the sentences. Use the correct form of the words in parentheses.

1 The University of the Arts in London ______________________________ (build) in 2008.

2 Air travel in Europe ______________________________ (affect) after a volcano in Iceland erupted in 2010.

3 Mount Trashmore in the United States was a landfill that ______________________________ (convert) into a park.

4 The Little Mermaid statue in Denmark ______________________________ (damage) a number of times since the 1960s.

F ▶ **5.8** Complete the information. Circle the correct words. Then listen and check your answers.

Cheonggyecheon is a stream that flows through the middle of Seoul, South Korea. But the 11-kilometer stream is very different from how it [1](**looked** / **has looked**) before—it [2](**is being transformed** / **has been transformed**) completely. Previously, the stream was covered by a large freeway. Then in 2003, the city government [3](**started** / **was started**) a huge project to restore it. The highway [4](**was removed** / **was being removed**), the stream [5](**is cleaned up** / **was cleaned up**), and the whole area was made into a park. Now, it [6](**is used** / **has been used**) by locals and tourists to relax and enjoy some greenery in the middle of the city.

Cheonggyecheon in Seoul, South Korea

SPEAKING Describing changes in my community

A How has your local community changed over time? Make a list of at least three ways in which it has changed.

B Create a simple timeline using the events you listed in **A**. Add details to each event.

C Work with a partner. Describe the changes in your community using your timeline. Give reasons for the changes and describe how you feel about them.

A few months ago, a new train station was built near my house, so …

My neighborhood wasn't really lively in the past, but recently a new shopping mall …

5C Barefoot College

PRE-READING Scanning

Scan the passage. Give an example of a skill that students learn at Barefoot College.

5.9

The Greek philosopher Aristotle once said, "For the things we have to learn before we can do them, we learn by doing them." This method of "learning by doing" has allowed Barefoot College to successfully train and educate millions of underprivileged people. Barefoot College was founded by Sanjit "Bunker" Roy. Shortly after graduating from Delhi University, Roy did some volunteer work in a poor region of India. The experience changed his life, and in 1972 he set up Barefoot College. His aim was to help rural[1] communities overcome their difficulties and become more independent.

Barefoot College is unlike any other college. All of its students around the world are from poor, rural communities. They don't have to be able to read or write—indeed, many can't. People of any age can attend—the school has a wide range of students, from children to grandmothers. The college is owned and managed by everyone who works and learns there. These "Barefoot Professionals" are trained to perform all sorts of duties in the school, from providing dental[2] care services to cooking meals for staff and students. No degrees or certificates are given out. But graduates return to their villages with their new skills and work to make their communities self-sufficient[3] by training other villagers. Being able to use their skills to serve their communities is **proof** of success.

The solar engineering program at Barefoot College has a **significant** role. Every year, the college **recruits** middle-aged women from rural villages that don't have electricity. For six months, the women learn how to build, install, use, and maintain solar lamps. The lack of a common language isn't a problem; they communicate through sign language and work with color-coded equipment. Through hands-on training, the women transform into solar engineers by the end of the program. The self-confidence they gain allows them to go on and inspire positive change in their villages. Since 2008, the women have managed to provide electricity to over 1,000 villages, bringing light to more than 40,000 households.

A student at Barefoot College builds a solar lamp.

Neema Gurung is one of the solar engineers at Barefoot College. With some financial help from the Indian government, she left her village in Nepal to take part in the program. As her village has no electricity, Gurung always had to finish her chores by sunset. For her, learning how to build solar lamps and bring light to her village will help greatly in **ensuring** the safety of her home. "Tigers often wander around our villages and have attacked locals in the past," Gurung explains. "It's like we are locked in our own house after darkness."

Barefoot College has demonstrated how education can empower rural people and help them live better lives. After its success in India, Barefoot College decided to expand its programs overseas. Today, it has a number of regional training centers in countries such as Ethiopia, Afghanistan, and Senegal. Through their hard work and **dedication**, thousands of Barefoot College graduates and teachers have transformed their communities into better places to live.

[1] **rural:** *adj.* of the countryside and not the city

[2] **dental:** *adj.* related to the teeth

[3] **self-sufficient:** *adj.* not requiring any form of help for survival

UNDERSTANDING MAIN IDEAS

Complete the profile of Barefoot College.

Barefoot College	
Founder	Sanjit "Bunker" Roy
Why was the college created?	While doing some [1] ______________ in a poor region of India, Roy was motivated to do something to help underprivileged communities.
Aim	The college was set up to help rural communities find solutions to their difficulties and become more [2] ______________.
How is it different from most other colleges?	• Students don't need to be able to [3] ______________. • There is no [4] ______________ limit. • No [5] ______________ are given out after students complete their training.

UNDERSTANDING DETAILS

Complete the sentences about the solar engineering program. Circle the correct words.

1 The solar engineering program mainly trains (**young women** / **middle-aged women**).

2 To overcome the language differences among students, the college uses (**sign language** / **illustrations**) and color-coded equipment in its training.

3 After the training, the women (**educate people in their village** / **receive a job recommendation letter**).

4 Neema Gurung hopes to improve the (**accessibility** / **safety**) of her village after training at Barefoot College.

BUILDING VOCABULARY

A Complete the sentences with the words from the box.

proof	significant	recruit	ensuring	dedication

1 The success of Barefoot College is ______________ that education can greatly improve the lives of rural people.

2 We need laws ______________ that the rights of the underprivileged are protected.

3 The ______________ of volunteers often inspires others to get involved.

4 Unlike most colleges, Barefoot College doesn't ______________ students based on academic grades.

5 Barefoot College makes a(n) ______________ difference to the lives of rural people by teaching them useful skills.

B CRITICAL THINKING

Reflecting Work with a partner. If you were able to interview Sanjit Roy to find out more about Barefoot College, what questions would you ask? Why?

5D How painting can transform communities

TEDTALKS

Artists **JEROEN KOOLHAAS** and **DRE URHAHN**—also known as Haas and Hahn—work on community projects in Rio de Janeiro. Seeing the **unfinished** buildings of the favelas—the crowded, **informal** neighborhoods of Rio de Janeiro—they worked with the locals to improve the community. Their **accomplishments** helped **transform** the favelas.

Haas and Hahn's idea worth spreading is that by bringing an entire community into the process of painting, neighborhoods can be transformed beautifully and residents benefit in ways far beyond what's visible.

PREVIEWING

Read the paragraphs above. Match each **bold** word to its meaning. You will hear these words in the TED Talk.

1 casual, not official ____________

2 incomplete ____________

3 successful achievements ____________

4 to change completely, usually for the better ____________

VIEWING

A ▶ 5.10 Watch Part 1 of the TED Talk. Answer questions 1 to 3.

1 Which of the following is true about Vila Cruzeiro?

  a It is located next to Copacabana Beach.

  b It was built largely by immigrants from Holland.

  c It is a community in the North Zone of Rio de Janeiro.

2 What surprised Haas and Hahn about the favelas?

  a Violent drug gangs live in the favelas.

  b The people who live in favelas are immigrants from the countryside.

  c The favelas were built without a master plan.

3 What made them want to start a painting project in the favelas?

a The locals asked them to paint their houses.

b They saw many unfinished houses.

c They were inspired by some of the local artwork.

B ▶ **5.11** Watch Part 2 of the TED Talk. Order the events describing Haas and Hahn's first project from 1–6.

__1__ Haas and Hahn told a friend about their idea.

_____ They installed a kite on the hill.

_____ The locals hated it.

_____ They painted a house blue.

_____ They painted an image of a boy.

_____ News articles were written about their work.

C ▶ **5.12** Watch Part 3 of the TED Talk. Circle **T** for true or **F** for false.

1	Haas and Hahn were asked to transform North Philly through painting.	**T**	**F**
2	They organized and sent a team of designers from Holland to North Philly.	**T**	**F**
3	A different design was made for every house.	**T**	**F**
4	Local people were trained as painters for the project.	**T**	**F**
5	Haas and Hahn want to bring their idea to other countries.	**T**	**F**

D **CRITICAL THINKING**

Synthesizing/Reflecting Work with a partner. How is Haas and Hahn's approach to helping communities similar to Martín Andrade's (page 65)? Which of these projects would you like to do in your community? Why?

VOCABULARY IN CONTEXT

A ▶ **5.13** Watch the excerpts from the TED Talk. Choose the correct meaning of the words.

B Complete the sentences with the words from the box.

emerge	notorious	install	approach	bottom-up

1 Crowdfunding is one ________________ to raising money for a good cause.

2 The favelas are ________________ for problems like crime and poverty.

3 The favelas were built from the ________________, without any master plan.

4 Sometimes, slums ________________ when a large number of people from the countryside move to the city.

5 Haas and Hahn's first project in Rio de Janeiro was to create and ________________ a piece of artwork in the favelas.

PRESENTATION SKILLS Ending with a hope for the future

> One way to make the end of your presentation memorable is to close with a comment that expresses your hope for the future. This encourages the audience to reflect on your topic.

A ▶ **5.14** Watch part of Haas and Hahn's TED Talk. What expression do they use to end their presentation?

a It's our dream that …

b We hope … maybe one day …

c We hope to see the world become …

B ▶ **5.15** Watch part of Kenneth Shinozuka's TED Talk. Complete the expression he uses to express his hope for the future.

"People living happily and healthily—that's ______________________________."

Haas and Hahn's painting project in Santa Marta, Rio de Janeiro

5E Proposing changes

COMMUNICATE A neighborhood survey

A Work with two classmates. You are going to conduct a survey about their neighborhoods. Ask the questions below and make notes. Ask follow-up questions to get more information.

Questions	Neighborhood: ______	Neighborhood: ______
1 How would you describe your neighborhood?		
2 What facilities does your community have?		
3 Which facilities do you use?		
4 What kinds of events are organized locally?		
5 Is there a sense of community in your neighborhood? If yes, what gives it a sense of community?		
6 What kinds of improvements would you like to see in your neighborhood?		

B In your group, brainstorm specific ideas to improve the neighborhoods above.

Making suggestions

It may be good to ... *Perhaps we could ...* *Why don't we ...* *One possible idea is ...*

The neighborhood could do with more bicycle lanes for cyclists …

We could help underprivileged children in our neighborhood by donating books …

WRITING Making a request

Write a short letter to your local government requesting a new feature, facility, or event for your neighborhood. Explain how it will help improve your community.

I'm writing to suggest creating a community garden in our neighborhood. There are many nature lovers in our community, so it would be a good place for people to gather …

A communal rooftop garden in Sydney, Australia

6 Clear Communication

"We desperately need great communication from our scientists and engineers."

Melissa Marshall
Communications teacher, TED speaker

UNIT GOALS

In this unit, you will ...

- talk about methods of communication.
- read about powerful ways to get your ideas across.
- watch a TED Talk about how complex ideas can be made easy to understand.

WARM UP

▶ 6.1 Watch part of Melissa Marshall's TED Talk. Answer the questions with a partner.

1 Why is good communication from scientists and engineers so important?

2 Look through the unit. What types of communication methods and strategies do you see?

Two customers chatting in a café in Italy

6A Good communication

VOCABULARY Using communication collocations

A Cross out the phrase that doesn't belong in each group.

1 have	a meeting	~~a post~~	a conversation
2 give	a text message	a report	a speech
3 make	a comment	a phone call	a letter
4 post	a letter	a text message	a comment
5 send	an email	a meeting	a document
6 share	a report	a comment	a phone call
7 write	a meeting	a blog	a message
8 check	an email	a phone call	a message

B Work with a partner. Write one more example for each word below.

1 have ____________________
2 give ____________________
3 make ____________________
4 post ____________________
5 send ____________________
6 share ____________________
7 write ____________________
8 check ____________________

C Work with a partner. Choose the communication method you prefer. Tell your partner why you prefer it.

1 writing an email OR writing a letter
2 making a phone call OR sending a text message
3 giving a speech OR writing a report

LISTENING Communication styles

Describing styles and preferences

Listen for phrases that show what the speaker prefers to do.

Generally, I prefer to …   *I usually try to …*   *I tend to …*

A ▶ 6.2 Watch author Neil Anderson talk about how he gives his presentations. Check (✓) the ways he prepares for them.

- ☐ He finds out about his audience.
- ☐ He calls teachers who are coming to his presentation.
- ☐ He makes sure he knows his presentation topic well.
- ☐ He prepares a list of useful reference materials.
- ☐ He creates slides.

Neil Anderson speaking to a group of teachers

B ▶ 6.2 Watch again. How does Anderson make his audience feel more involved in his presentations? Discuss with a partner.

C **CRITICAL THINKING**

Reflecting Work with a partner. Which of Anderson's methods would you use if you gave a presentation? Why?

SPEAKING Talking about communication preferences

A ▶ 6.3 If you need to get in touch with Speaker B, what is the best way to contact him?

A: Hey, did you see the message I sent you on Facebook yesterday?

B: Sorry, I don't often log in to check my Facebook account—I prefer talking on the phone. Was it something urgent?

A: Oh, not really. I just wanted to ask you to upload the photos from the party the other day.

B: Oh, sure. I'll do that tomorrow after I'm done working on my presentation.

A: Thanks. Is the presentation for that science project you mentioned?

B: Yeah, it is. So I'll probably be pretty busy today. You should call if you need me.

A: OK. Good luck with your presentation!

B Practice the conversation with a partner.

C Work with a partner. Talk about the communication methods or tools you frequently use. Use the expressions in blue above to help you.

How often do you check your Facebook account?

Not very often. I prefer texting. What about you?

I log in to Facebook every day. I use it to …

6B How do you communicate?

LANGUAGE FOCUS Describing types of communicators

A 6.4 Read about the four types of communicators below. Which do you think you are? Look at the flowchart on page 171 and find out.

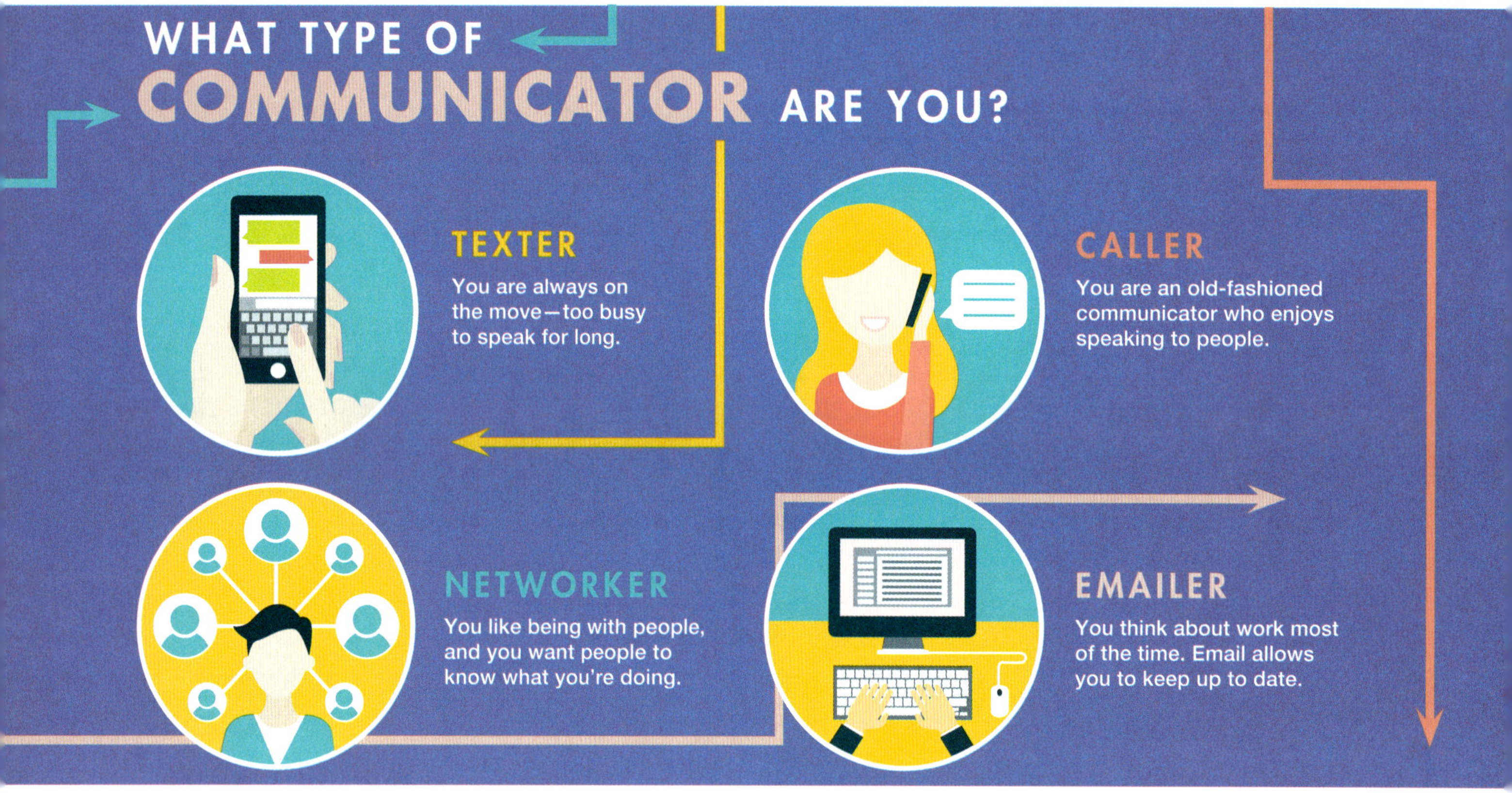

B 6.5 Listen to the conversation. What kind of communicators described in **A** do you think the two speakers are?

Jon: ____________________ Mel: ____________________

C 6.6 Watch and study the language in the chart.

Talking about communication preferences	
I generally	avoid texting people. hate calling people. recommend posting a comment online.
She	tries to call her parents every week. prefers to use social media to connect with people. promised to send a postcard.
Social networking allows me to keep in touch with my friends. I don't like my friends to text me. Video calling helps me (to) stay in touch with my family.	

For more information on **verb patterns with -ing and infinitive**, see Grammar Summary 6 on pages 185–186.

D ▶ 6.5 Listen to the conversation in **B** again. Complete the sentences from the conversation.

1 "I much prefer ________________ to people."

2 "I usually ________________ because people are always busy and they never answer."

E Find and correct the mistake in each sentence. Do you agree with the statements? Tell a partner the reasons for your answers.

1 It may be stressful, but we should all learn how to speaking in public.

2 I think that use social media is a waste of time.

3 The government should try to persuade people being polite online.

4 I prefer to emailing over talking on the phone.

5 To text encourages us to be lazy writers.

6 It's better to call someone than text them when you want asking for help.

F ▶ 6.7 Complete the information. Circle the correct words. Then listen and check your answers.

Many people worry that [1](**to text** / **texting**) will make people [2](**to forget** / **forget**) how to write well. This isn't a new concern. Throughout history, people have always complained about young people [3](**to use** / **using**) incorrect grammar. In fact, more than 2,000 years ago, there were already complaints about people [4](**using** / **use**) bad Latin! Some language experts believe that texting is actually a new kind of language—it allows us [5](**to write** / **write**) more like the way we speak.

Texting is one of the main modes of communication for many teens today.

SPEAKING Communication methods

Work with a partner. What methods of communication do you think are most appropriate for the situations below? Why?

1 Two of your friends are getting married. You'd like to congratulate them.

2 You need to apologize to a customer for sending the wrong information.

3 You have to tell your employees that they are going to lose their jobs because the office is closing.

4 You are not happy in your current relationship. You have decided you are going to break it off.

I think the best way to congratulate my friends would be to send them a card because ...

I think it's better to call them because ...

6C Communication in the digital age

PRE-READING Reflecting

Work with a partner. Have you seen or heard a speech recently that you really enjoyed? What did you like most about it?

▶ 6.8

We live in an age of information overload.[1] Research shows that the average social media user receives about 300 pieces of content a day—roughly equivalent to the number of words in a standard novel. With such a huge amount of content available, people are likely to spend less time going through each piece of information. Therefore, data has to be delivered quickly and effectively in order to grab people's attention.

SEVEN WAYS TO COMMUNICATE MORE EFFECTIVELY

Here are some suggestions on ways we can engage our audience in our writing and during presentations:

Use subheadings. They allow you to group your ideas and guide your readers.

Describe your ideas in a simple way. To test whether your description is simple enough, try explaining it to someone who knows nothing about your topic. But make sure that you keep the essential parts—avoid dumbing ideas down until they lose their meaning.

Present ideas logically and concisely. Use clear language and avoid **technical** words.

Include stories. Personal stories can provide a human connection and make your point more memorable.

Give analogies. They help to make complex ideas meaningful. For example, you could describe electricity as water flowing through a pipe.

ONLINE STRATEGIES

According to a 2015 study by Microsoft, the average Internet user is estimated to have an attention **span** of about eight seconds—even shorter than that of a goldfish! Other research also shows that one in three users will switch websites if the page doesn't load within five seconds. So how can writers keep online readers' attention and interest? Below are a few things to note for online communication:

- **Highlight your main goal right at the start**—grab the viewer's attention immediately with a short and clear message.
- **Use bullet points** to reduce the amount of text and focus attention on the most important details.
- **Ensure that pages load fast.** There are many web resources that can analyze websites and suggest ways to make them faster.
- **Avoid cluttering[2] the page**—less is definitely more when it comes to web design.

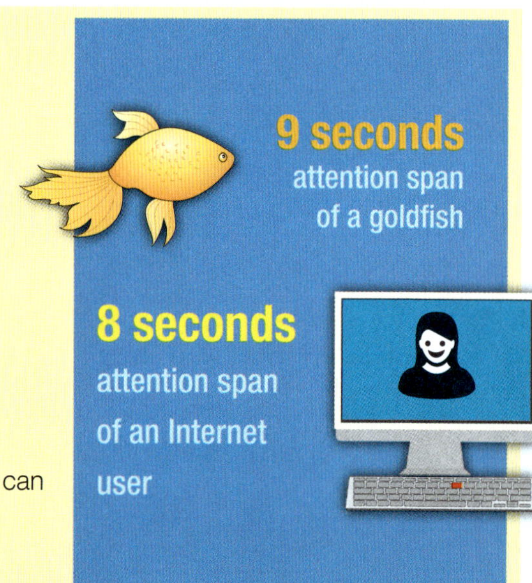

A commuter reading on her phone on a crowded train in Hong Kong

Use quotes. They are often interesting ways to start or end a presentation, and can be a source of humor.

Use attractive visuals. Visual aids such as photographs, diagrams, and charts can appeal directly to your audience's imagination and create a more **lasting** impact.

GETTING OUR IDEAS ACROSS

Gone are the days when only a select few could share their ideas with a wide audience. Today, modern technology allows anyone to reach a wide audience. Now that we have this power, it is even more important that we learn to present our thoughts clearly and effectively in the digital age.

[1] **overload:** *n.* too much of something
[2] **clutter:** *v.* to fill something in a messy way

UNDERSTANDING MAIN IDEAS

What is the main purpose of the passage?

a to explain how technology helps us communicate
b to suggest ways to increase people's attention span
c to discuss how we can get our ideas across effectively

UNDERSTANDING DETAILS

A Choose the correct options.

1 The Online Strategies section gives data on our attention spans to show that ______.
  a people have become slower at reading
  b websites need to engage readers very quickly
  c more people prefer to get information online

2 Which of the following is the author likely to agree with?
  a Social media sites are becoming reliable sources of information.
  b Online content writers tend to focus more on text than design.
  c With access to technology, people can now reach out to a very wide audience.

B Match the sentences to the communication tips that they illustrate.

1 Look at the Venn diagram on the screen. ○	○ Include stories.
2 This reminds me of a challenge I faced in my youth. ○	○ Give analogies.
3 The human liver is like a chemical factory. ○	○ Use quotes.
4 As John F. Kennedy once said, "Ask not what your country can do for you, ask what you can do for your country." ○	○ Use attractive visuals.

BUILDING VOCABULARY

A Complete the sentences using the correct form of the words in blue from the passage.

1 The average human life ______________ has increased greatly over the last 100 years.
2 Learning how to write ______________ is one of the most important skills for a writer.
3 Don't complicate your essay with too many ______________ terms.
4 The treatment had a(n) ______________ effect on me—I no longer get backaches.
5 Comparing the human brain to a computer can be a good ______________ for describing how the brain works.

B CRITICAL THINKING

Evaluating Look at the passage again. Choose three ideas for effective communication that you think are important. Explain your choices to a partner.

6D Talk nerdy to me

TEDTALKS

MELISSA MARSHALL works at the Department of Communication Arts & Sciences at Penn State University. She specializes in teaching speaking skills to engineering students.

Melissa Marshall's idea worth spreading is that even complex and technical topics can be easy to understand and exciting if they are communicated in the right ways.

PREVIEWING

Read the paragraph below. Match each **bold** word to its meaning. You will hear these words in the TED Talk.

Melissa Marshall believes that we **desperately** need great communication from our scientists and engineers. This is because scientists **tackle** some of the world's biggest problems—like climate change. While it is important for scientists to make everyone understand their work, Marshall points out that they must not **dumb down** their ideas. Scientists need to communicate their ideas without **compromising** them. Marshall also recommends that scientists use stories to **engage** us and get us excited.

1. making something weaker ____________
2. to make something too simple ____________
3. to form a connection with ____________
4. seriously; urgently ____________
5. to deal with (a problem) ____________

VIEWING

A ▶ 6.9 Watch Part 1 of the TED Talk. Choose the correct options.

1. What analogy does Marshall use?
   - **a** an animal
   - **b** a fantasy story
2. Why do you think she makes this analogy?
   - **a** to describe how unfamiliar the situation was for her
   - **b** to describe how exciting the situation was
3. What is the amazing new world that Marshall wants us to see?
   - **a** the ideas that scientists and engineers have
   - **b** the lives of scientists and engineers

B ▶ **6.10** Watch Part 2 of the TED Talk. Check (✓) the advice that Marshall has for scientists and engineers.

- ☐ Show how science is relevant to non-scientists.
- ☐ Give demonstrations where possible.
- ☐ Avoid using jargon when speaking.
- ☐ Simplify ideas as much as possible.
- ☐ Don't use bullet points in presentations.
- ☐ Use less text and more visuals on slides.

C ▶ **6.11** Watch Part 3 of the TED Talk. Discuss these questions with a partner.

1. Why do you think Marshall uses an equation to summarize her talk? What do you think it means?
2. Can you think of another technique she could have used to end her presentation in a memorable way?

D CRITICAL THINKING

Evaluating/Synthesizing Discuss these questions with a partner.

1. Look at the photo at the bottom of the page. Do you like it? How effective do you think it is as a way of communicating information?
2. Compare Marshall's recommendations with the advice in the reading on pages 80–81. How similar are they?

An infographic on a Kulula Airlines plane

VOCABULARY IN CONTEXT

A ▶ **6.12** Watch the excerpts from the TED Talk. Choose the correct meaning of the words.

B Complete the sentences using the words in the box.

beware of	barriers to	key into	by all means

1 Keep your presentation slides simple to allow the audience to ________________ the main point on each slide.

2 When making online purchases, you need to ________________ hidden costs.

3 Language differences are not necessarily ________________ intercultural understanding—we can learn about other cultures through music, food, or art.

4 If you feel confident, ________________ apply for the job.

PRESENTATION SKILLS Engaging with your audience

Make your presentation seem like a conversation in order to connect with your audience. Here are some ways you can do this:

- Make eye contact.
- Use relaxed and friendly body language.
- Talk enthusiastically—let your personality come through.

A ▶ **6.13** Watch part of Melissa Marshall's TED Talk. Check (✓) the techniques that she uses.

Melissa Marshall ______.

☐ speaks energetically

☐ asks the audience questions

☐ smiles and uses humor

☐ gets someone to join her onstage

☐ is relaxed while presenting

☐ checks her audience's understanding before continuing

B Work with a partner. What advantages are there to making a presentation like a conversation?

I think a presentation that feels like a conversation allows the audience to relax while listening.

C Work in groups. Brainstorm other ways to make a presentation feel like a conversation.

6E Simplifying ideas

COMMUNICATE Explaining a topic of interest

A You are going to explain a particular idea or concept. It can be a game, a sport, a hobby, or an idea from your work or study. Choose a topic and write some notes on it below.

My topic:

Key points:

B Decide how you will explain the topic. Think about how you can make it easy to understand.

Giving an explanation

I'd like to tell you more about …	*… is like a(n) …*
The basic idea of … is …	*You can think of it as a(n) …*

C Work in groups. Take turns explaining your topic to your group members.

WRITING Giving an explanation

Choose one of the topics that your group members talked about. Write a paragraph about what it is and what you learned about it.

One of my group members talked about ice hockey. It's a sport that's popular in parts of North America and Europe. There are six players on each team, including one goaltender. The aim is to score more points than the other team by …

A player scores in an ice hockey match.

Presentation 2

MODEL PRESENTATION

A Complete the transcript of the presentation using the words in the box.

better	**to share**	**upload**	**submit**
app	**are fixed**	**more efficient**	**most important**

Hi, I'm Scott. It's great to be here today. Tell me, how many of you have noticed a problem in your neighborhood, like broken street lights? Right, most of you. And how many of you reported it to the local government? Hmm, nobody. Today, I'm going to explain a simple idea that can help people improve their neighborhood.

My idea is for an [1]__________________, which allows you [2]__________________ and report local issues. Imagine you're walking down the street and you find a tree blocking the way or trash dumped in a park. You take some photos and open up the app. You [3]__________________ the photo and add any comments you want. Everyone can then see the details on a map. You can see the issues that people report and when they [4]__________________. Here, you can see the photo of the problem and the location on the map. And here is a list of things that people can [5]__________________. But that's not all. Users can vote on the [6]__________________ issues and which should be fixed first. So we all help to improve the local area as well as make the government [7]__________________.

So, that's my idea for how we can all help make our neighborhoods [8]__________________. Actually, there are some cities around the world doing this already. My hope is that the idea will spread to all our neighborhoods, so we can all enjoy a more pleasant and safe environment. Thank you for listening.

B ▶ **P.2** Watch the presentation and check your answers.

C ▶ **P.2** Review the list of presentation skills from Units 1–6 below. Which does the speaker use? Check (✓) them as you watch again. Then compare with a partner.

The speaker …

- helps the audience visualize by
  - doing a demonstration ☐
  - giving interesting facts ☐
  - telling a story ☐
  - using visuals ☐
- comments on visuals ☐
- opens with an interesting fact ☐
- asks the audience questions ☐
- ends with a hope for the future ☐
- engages with the audience ☐

YOUR TURN

A You are going to plan and give a short presentation to explain an idea for improving communication among residents and strengthening the local sense of community. Think about how you could use technology to help the community connect with each other. Make notes in the chart below.

How do people in your neighborhood communicate with one another now?
How close are people in your neighborhood?
How can technology help to improve communication?

B Look at the useful phrases in the box below. Think about which ones you will need in your presentation.

Useful phrases

Asking the audience questions:	*What do you think of when …?* *How many of you …?*
Making suggestions:	*My idea is for a/an … that …* *What I'd like to propose is …* *One way to improve communication is …*
Describing communities:	*tight-knit, supportive, united*

C Work with a partner. Take turns giving your presentation using your notes. Use some of the presentation skills from Units 1–6 below. As you listen, check (✓) each skill your partner uses.

The speaker …

- helps the audience visualize by
  - doing a demonstration ☐
  - giving interesting facts ☐
  - telling a story ☐
  - using visuals ☐
- comments on visuals ☐
- opens with an interesting fact ☐
- asks the audience questions ☐
- ends with a hope for the future ☐
- engages with the audience ☐

D Give your partner some feedback on their talk. Include at least two things you liked and one thing that could be improved.

> I liked your presentation. You asked questions and shared an interesting story. But the end of your talk was a bit abrupt.

Communication Activities

2E COMMUNICATE

STUDENT A

Read the information below. Then explain to your partner what the innovation is.

Food-scanning technology

What it is

This technology allows you to use devices called food scanners to check the nutritional details of the food you're eating.

How it works

The device scans food and analyzes its chemical breakdown. It then sends detailed information about the food item, such as the amount of calories, proteins, or fat, to an app on your smartphone.

How this changes things

- People don't have to spend time examining food labels to find out if the food contains anything they can't eat or don't want to eat.
- People can keep track of what they eat more accurately.

3B SPEAKING

STUDENT A

Read the information below. Make notes or highlight key words. Then describe the technology to your partner and explain the effects it could have on people in the future.

Sensors that you can eat

What are they?

These are small monitoring devices in the form of medicine pills. Once eaten, these devices monitor your body and send information wirelessly to your smartphone or computer.

Examples of potential benefits

- Patients can easily monitor their health.
- Doctors could use the data to decide on the most suitable treatment for a patient. Patients don't have to visit the hospital for physical checkups.
- Medical researchers could gather data on patients with similar health conditions or illnesses to find cures.

As edible sensors are able to constantly monitor your health, doctors can …

2E COMMUNICATE

STUDENT B

Read the information below. Then explain to your partner what the innovation is.

Mobile payment technology

What it is

This technology allows you to use mobile phones to pay for all kinds of things.

How it works

Users create an account on an app on their smartphones. They then store their credit card details in the app.

How this changes things

- People won't have to carry around bulky wallets or worry about forgetting to take their loyalty/rewards card with them.
- It will be easier to split payments when you're eating or shopping with a group of people.
- Shops can use the data from mobile payments to offer customers personalized deals.

3B SPEAKING

STUDENT B

Read the information below. Make notes or highlight key words. Then describe the technology to your partner and explain the effects it could have on people in the future.

3-D printers for body parts

What are they?

These are machines that can print various parts of our body such as skin, bone, or organs. 3-D printers already exist, but they are not yet being widely used for healthcare purposes.

Examples of potential benefits

- Patients who need organ donations don't have to wait for suitable donors.
- Patients with burns or skin diseases can replace the affected areas with new skin.
- We could create new bones for people suffering from bone-related diseases or who have serious injuries.

3-D printers are very useful for healthcare because they may be able to quickly produce …

4B SPEAKING

	Virtual reality (VR) headset 1	Virtual reality (VR) headset 2
Platform	Smartphone	Computer
Price	$250	$700
Weight	320 g	650 g
Plays 3-D games	Yes	Yes
Plays 3-D movies	No	Yes
Connects to social media	No	Yes
Pros	• Quick set-up • Comfortable to wear • Easy to use	• Amazing picture quality • Has augmented reality* technology • Can be used with educational software
Cons	• Average picture quality • Limited number of games available • Games take a while to load	• Bulky • Takes a while to set up and learn how to use • Can cause motion sickness in some users
Rating (1–5 stars)	★★★	★★★★

***Augmented reality:** You see both the virtual world and the real world through the headset. You are able to interact with virtual contents in the real world, and distinguish between the two.

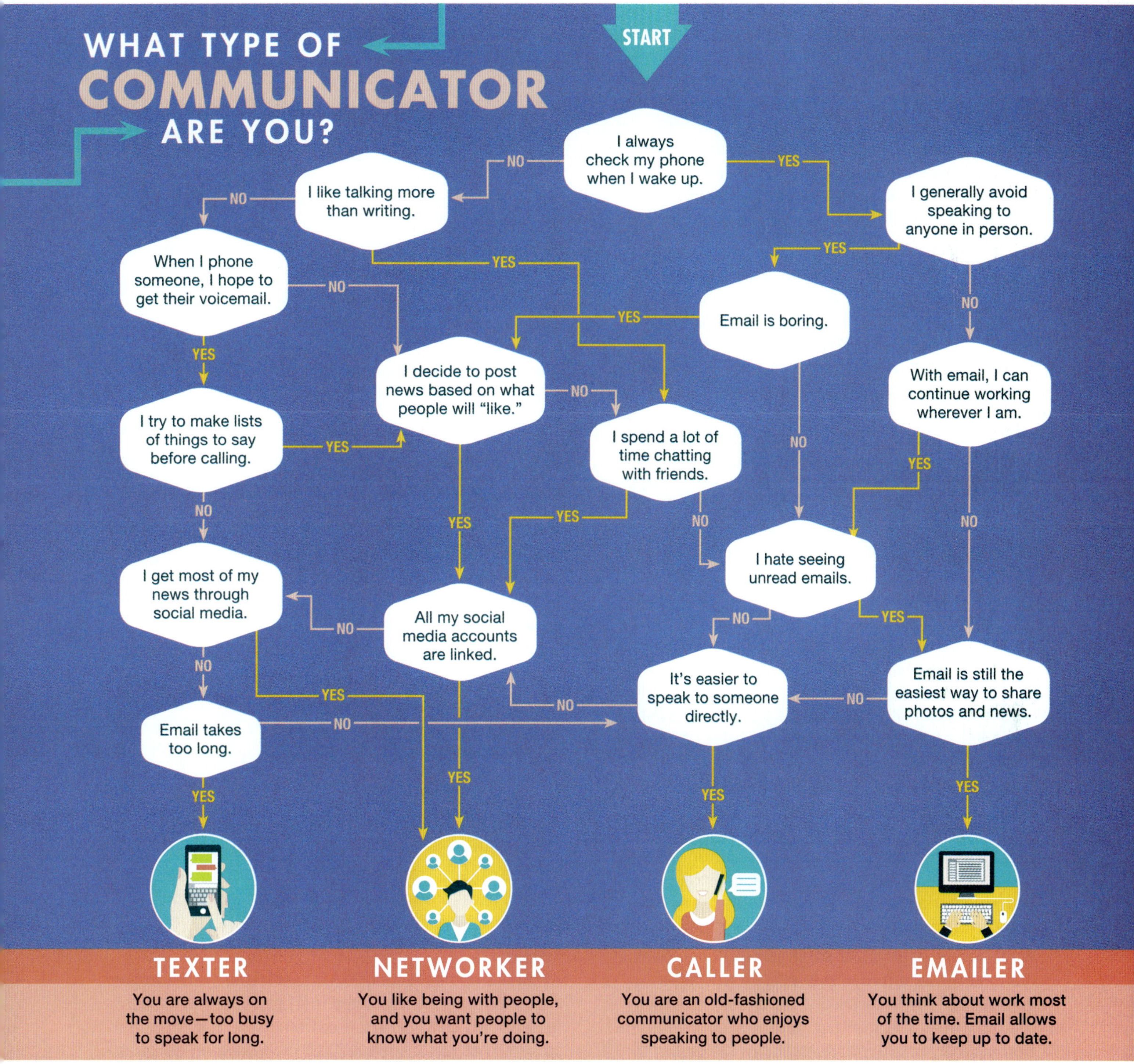
WHAT TYPE OF COMMUNICATOR ARE YOU?
START
I always check my phone when I wake up.
I like talking more than writing.
I generally avoid speaking to anyone in person.
When I phone someone, I hope to get their voicemail.
Email is boring.
I decide to post news based on what people will "like."
With email, I can continue working wherever I am.
I try to make lists of things to say before calling.
I spend a lot of time chatting with friends.
I get most of my news through social media.
I hate seeing unread emails.
All my social media accounts are linked.
It's easier to speak to someone directly.
Email is still the easiest way to share photos and news.
Email takes too long.
YES
NO
TEXTER
You are always on the move—too busy to speak for long.
NETWORKER
You like being with people, and you want people to know what you're doing.
CALLER
You are an old-fashioned communicator who enjoys speaking to people.
EMAILER
You think about work most of the time. Email allows you to keep up to date.

TED Talk Transcripts

Unit 1 Mark Bezos: A life lesson from a volunteer firefighter

Part 1

Back in New York, I am the head of development for a non-profit called Robin Hood. When I'm not fighting poverty, I'm fighting fires as the assistant captain of a volunteer fire company. Now in our town, where the volunteers supplement a highly skilled career staff, you have to get to the fire scene pretty early to get in on any action.

I remember my first fire. I was the second volunteer on the scene, so there was a pretty good chance I was going to get in. But still it was a real footrace against the other volunteers to get to the captain in charge to find out what our assignments would be. When I found the captain, he was having a very engaging conversation with the homeowner, who was surely having one of the worst days of her life. Here it was, the middle of the night, she was standing outside in the pouring rain, under an umbrella, in her pajamas, barefoot, while her house was in flames.

Part 2

The other volunteer who had arrived just before me—let's call him Lex Luthor—(Laughter) got to the captain first and was asked to go inside and save the homeowner's dog. The dog! I was stunned with jealousy. Here was some lawyer or money manager who, for the rest of his life, gets to tell people that he went into a burning building to save a living creature, just because he beat me by five seconds. Well, I was next. The captain waved me over. He said, "Bezos, I need you to go into the house. I need you to go upstairs, past the fire, and I need you to get this woman a pair of shoes." (Laughter) I swear. So, not exactly what I was hoping for, but off I went—up the stairs, down the hall, past the "real" firefighters, who were pretty much done putting out the fire at this point, into the master bedroom to get a pair of shoes.

Now I know what you're thinking, but I'm no hero. (Laughter) I carried my payload back downstairs where I met my nemesis and the precious dog by the front door. We took our treasures outside to the homeowner, where, not surprisingly, his received much more attention than did mine. A few weeks later, the department received a letter from the homeowner thanking us for the valiant effort displayed in saving her home. The act of kindness she noted above all others: someone had even gotten her a pair of shoes.

(Laughter)

Part 3

In both my vocation at Robin Hood and my avocation as a volunteer firefighter, I am witness to acts of generosity and kindness on a monumental scale, but I'm also witness to acts of grace and courage on an individual basis. And you know what I've learned? They all matter. So as I look around this room at people who either have achieved, or are on their way to achieving, remarkable levels of success, I would offer this reminder: don't wait. Don't wait until you make your first million to make a difference in somebody's life. If you have something to give, give it now. Serve food at a soup kitchen. Clean up a neighborhood park. Be a mentor.

Not every day is going to offer us a chance to save somebody's life, but every day offers us an opportunity to affect one. So get in the game. Save the shoes.

Thank you.

Unit 2 Derek Sivers: How to start a movement

Part 1

So, ladies and gentlemen, at TED we talk a lot about leadership and how to make a movement. So let's watch a movement happen, start to finish, in under three minutes and dissect some lessons from it.

First, of course you know, a leader needs the guts to stand out and be ridiculed. But what he's doing is so easy to follow. So here's his first follower with a crucial role; he's going to show everyone else how to follow.

Now, notice that the leader embraces him as an equal. So, now it's not about the leader anymore; it's about them, plural. Now, there he is calling to his friends. Now, if you notice that the first follower is actually an underestimated form of leadership in itself. It takes guts to stand out like that. The first follower is what transforms a lone nut into a leader. (Laughter) (Applause)

Part 2

And here comes a second follower. Now it's not a lone nut, it's not two nuts—three is a crowd, and a crowd is news. So a movement must be public. It's important to show not just the leader, but the followers, because you find that new followers emulate the followers, not the leader.

Now, here come two more people, and immediately after, three more people. Now we've got momentum. This is the tipping point. Now we've got a movement. So, notice that, as more people join in, it's less risky.

So those that were sitting on the fence before, now have no reason not to. They won't stand out, they won't be ridiculed, but they will be part of the in-crowd if they hurry. (Laughter) So, over the next minute, you'll see all of those that prefer to stick with the crowd because eventually they would be ridiculed for not joining in. And that's how you make a movement.

Part 3

But let's recap some lessons from this. So first, if you are the type, like the shirtless dancing guy that is standing alone, remember the importance of nurturing your first few followers as equals so it's clearly about the movement, not you. OK, but we might have missed the real lesson here.

The biggest lesson, if you noticed—did you catch it?—is that leadership is over-glorified. That, yes, it was the shirtless guy who was first, and he'll get all the credit, but it was really the first follower that transformed the lone nut into a leader. So, as we're told that we should all be leaders, that would be really ineffective.

If you really care about starting a movement, have the courage to follow and show others how to follow. And when you find a lone nut doing something great, have the guts to be the first one to stand up and join in. And what a perfect place to do that, at TED.

Thanks. (Applause)

Unit 3 Kenneth Shinozuka: My simple invention, designed to keep my grandfather safe

Part 1

What's the fastest growing threat to Americans' health? Cancer? Heart attacks? Diabetes? The answer is actually none of these; it's Alzheimer's disease. Every 67 seconds, someone in the United States is diagnosed with Alzheimer's. As the number of Alzheimer's patients triples by the year 2050, caring for them, as well as the rest of the aging population, will become an overwhelming societal challenge.

My family has experienced firsthand the struggles of caring for an Alzheimer's patient. Growing up in a family with three generations, I've always been very close to my grandfather. When I was four years old, my grandfather and I were walking in a park in Japan when he suddenly got lost. It was one of the scariest moments I've ever experienced in my life, and it was also the first instance that informed us that my grandfather had Alzheimer's disease. Over the past 12 years, his condition got worse and worse, and his wandering in particular caused my family a lot of stress. My aunt, his primary caregiver, really struggled to stay awake at night to keep an eye on him, and even then often failed to catch him leaving the bed. I became really concerned about my aunt's well-being as well as my grandfather's safety. I searched extensively for a solution that could help my family's problems, but couldn't find one.

Part 2

Then, one night about two years ago, I was looking after my grandfather and I saw him stepping out of the bed. The moment his foot landed on the floor, I thought, why don't I put a pressure sensor on the heel of his foot? Once he stepped onto the floor and out of the bed, the pressure sensor would detect an increase in pressure caused by body weight and then wirelessly send an audible alert to the caregiver's smartphone. That way, my aunt could sleep much better at night without having to worry about my grandfather's wandering.

So now I'd like to perform a demonstration of the sock. Could I please have my sock model on stage? Great. So once the patient steps onto the floor—(Ringing)—an alert is sent to the caregiver's smartphone.

Thank you. (Applause)

Thank you, sock model.

So this is a drawing of my preliminary design.

My desire to create a sensor-based technology perhaps stemmed from my lifelong love for sensors and technology. When I was six years old, an elderly family friend fell down in the bathroom and suffered severe injuries. I became concerned about my own grandparents and decided to invent a smart bathroom system. Motion sensors would be installed inside the tiles of bathroom floors to detect the falls of elderly patients whenever they fell down in the bathroom. Since I was only six years old at the time and I hadn't graduated from kindergarten yet, I didn't have the necessary resources and tools to translate my idea into reality, but nonetheless, my research experience really implanted in me a firm desire to use sensors to help the elderly people. I really believe that sensors can improve the quality of life of the elderly.

Part 3

[. . .] I've tested the device on my grandfather for about a year now, and it's had a 100 percent success rate in detecting the over 900 known cases of his wandering. Last summer, I was able to beta test my device at several residential care facilities in California, and I'm currently incorporating the feedback to further improve the device into a marketable product. Testing the device on a number of patients made me realize that I needed to invent solutions for people who didn't want to wear socks to sleep at night.

So sensor data, collected on a vast number of patients, can be useful for improving patient care and also leading to a cure for the disease, possibly. For example, I'm currently examining correlations between the frequency of a patient's nightly wandering and his or her daily activities and diet.

One thing I'll never forget is when my device first caught my grandfather's wandering out of bed at night. At that moment, I was really struck by the power of technology to change lives for the better. People living happily and healthily—that's the world that I imagine.

Thank you very much.

(Applause)

Unit 4 Margaret Gould Stewart: How giant websites design for you (and a billion others, too)

Part 1

What do you think of when I say the word "design"? You probably think of things like this: finely crafted objects that you can hold in your hand, or maybe logos and posters and maps that visually explain things, classic icons of timeless design. But I'm not here to talk about that kind of design. I want to talk about the kind that you probably use every day and may not give much thought to, designs that change all the time and that live inside your pocket. I'm talking about the design of digital experiences and specifically the design of systems that are so big that their scale can be hard to comprehend. Consider the fact that Google processes over one billion search queries every day, that every minute, over 100 hours of footage are uploaded to YouTube. That's more in a single day than all three major U.S. networks broadcast in the last five years combined. And Facebook transmitting the photos, messages, and stories of over 1.23 billion people. That's almost half of the Internet population, and a sixth of humanity.

These are some of the products that I've helped design over the course of my career, and their scale is so massive that they've produced unprecedented design challenges. But what is really hard about designing at scale is this: It's hard in part because it requires a combination of two things, audacity and humility—audacity to believe that the thing that you're making is something that the entire world wants and needs, and humility to understand that as a designer, it's not about you or your portfolio, it's about the people that you're designing for, and how your work just might help them live better lives. Now, unfortunately, there's no school that offers the course Designing for Humanity 101. I and the other designers who work on these kinds of products have had to kind of invent it as we go along, and we are teaching ourselves the emerging best practices of designing at scale, and today I'd like to share some of the things that we've learned over the years.

Part 2

Now, the first thing that you need to know about designing at scale is that the little things really matter. Here's a really good example of how a very tiny design element can make a big impact. Now, the team at Facebook that manages the Facebook "Like" button decided that it needed to be redesigned. The button had kind of gotten out of sync with the evolution of our brand and it needed to be modernized. Now you might think, well, it's a tiny little button, it probably is a pretty straightforward, easy design assignment, but it wasn't. Turns out, there were all kinds of constraints for the design of this button. You had to work within specific height and width parameters. You had to be careful to make it work in a bunch of different languages, and be careful about using fancy gradients or borders because it has to degrade gracefully in old web browsers. The truth is, designing this tiny little button was a huge pain in the butt.

Now, this is the new version of the button, and the designer who led this project estimates that he spent over 280 hours redesigning this button over the course of months. Now, why would we spend so much time on something so small? It's because when you're designing at scale, there's no such thing as a small detail. This innocent little button is seen on average 22 billion times a day and on over 7.5 million websites. It's one of the single most viewed design elements ever created. Now that's a lot of pressure for a little button and the designer behind it, but with these kinds of products, you need to get even the tiny things right.

Part 3

[. . .] Now, when you set a goal to design for the entire human race, and you start to engage in that goal in earnest, at some point you run into the walls of the bubble that you're living in. Now, in San Francisco, we get a little miffed when we hit a dead cell zone because we can't use our phones to navigate to the new hipster coffee shop. But what if you had to drive four hours to charge your phone because you had no reliable source of electricity? What if you had no access to public libraries? What if your country had no free press? What would these products start to mean to you? This is what Google, YouTube, and Facebook look like to most of the world, and it's what they'll look like to most of the next five billion people to come online. Designing for low-end cell phones is not glamorous design work, but if you want to design for the whole world, you have to design for where people are, and not where you are.

So how do we keep this big, big picture in mind? We try to travel outside of our bubble to see, hear, and understand the people we're designing for. We use our products in non-English languages to make sure that they work just as well. And we try to use one of these phones from time to time to keep in touch with their reality.

So what does it mean to design at a global scale? It means difficult and sometimes exasperating work to try to improve and evolve products. Finding the audacity and the humility to do right by them can be pretty exhausting, and the humility part, it's a little tough on the design ego. Because these products are always changing, everything that I've designed in my career is pretty much gone, and everything that I will design will fade away. But here's what remains: the never-ending thrill of being a part of something that is so big, you can hardly get your head around it, and the promise that it just might change the world.

Thank you.

(Applause)

Unit 5 Haas and Hahn: How painting can transform communities

Part 1

Dre Urhahn: This theater is built on Copacabana, which is the most famous beach in the world. But 25 kilometers away from here in the North Zone of Rio lies a community called Vila Cruzeiro, and roughly 60,000 people live there. Now, the people here in Rio mostly know Vila Cruzeiro from the news, and unfortunately, news from Vila Cruzeiro often is not good news. But Vila Cruzeiro is also the place where our story begins.

Jeroen Koolhaas: Ten years ago, we first came to Rio to shoot a documentary about life in the favelas. Now, we learned that favelas are informal communities. They emerged over the years when immigrants from the countryside came to the cities looking for work, like cities within the cities, known for problems with crime, poverty, and the violent drug war between police and the drug gangs. So what struck us was that these were communities that the people who lived there had built with their own hands, without a master plan and like a giant work in progress. Where we're from, in Holland, everything is planned. We even have rules for how to follow the rules. (Laughter)

DU: So the last day of filming, we ended up in Vila Cruzeiro, and we were sitting down and we had a drink, and we were overlooking this hill with all these houses, and most of these houses looked unfinished, and they had walls of bare brick, but we saw some of these houses that were plastered and painted, and suddenly we had this idea: what would it look like if all these houses would be plastered and painted? And then we imagined one big design, one big work of art. Who would expect something like that in a place like this? So we thought, would that even be possible?

Part 2

[. . .] JK: We had a friend. He ran an NGO in Vila Cruzeiro. His name was Nanko, and he also liked the idea. He said, "You know, everybody here would pretty much love to have their houses plastered and painted. It's when a house is finished." So he introduced us to the right people, and Vitor and Maurinho became our crew. We picked three houses in the center of the community and we start here. We made a few designs, and everybody liked this design of a boy flying a kite the best. So we started painting, and the first thing we did was to paint everything blue, and we thought that looked already pretty good. But they hated it. The people who lived there really hated it. They said, "What did you do? You painted our house in exactly the same color as the police station." (Laughter) In a favela, that is not a good thing. Also the same color as the prison cell. So we quickly went ahead and we painted the boy, and then we thought we were finished, we were really happy, but still, it wasn't good because the little kids started coming up to us, and they said, "You know, there's a boy flying the kite, but where is his kite?" We said, "Uh, it's art. You know, you have to imagine the kite." (Laughter) And they said, "No, no, no, we want to see the kite." So we quickly installed a kite way up high on the hill, so that you could see the boy flying the kite and you could actually see a kite. So the local news started writing about it, which was great, and then even The Guardian wrote about it: "Notorious slum becomes open-air gallery."

Part 3

[. . .] DU: So then we received an unexpected phone call from the Philadelphia Mural Arts Program, and they had this question if this idea, our approach, if this would actually work in North Philly, which is one of the poorest neighborhoods in the United States. So we immediately said yes. We had no idea how, but it seemed like a very interesting challenge, so we did exactly the same as we did in Rio, and we moved into the neighborhood and started barbecuing. (Laughter) So the project took almost two years to complete, and we made individual designs for every single house on the avenue that we painted, and we made these designs together with the local store owners, the building owners, and a team of about a dozen young men and women. They were hired, and then they were trained as painters, and together they transformed their own neighborhood, the whole street, into a giant patchwork of color. (Applause) And at the end, the city of Philadelphia thanked every single one of them and gave them like a merit for their accomplishment.

[. . .] DU: So while this is happening, we are bringing this idea all over the world. So, like the project we did in Philadelphia, we are also invited to do workshops, for instance in Curaçao, and right now we're planning a huge project in Haiti.

JK: So the favela was not only the place where this idea started: it was also the place that made it possible to work without a master plan, because these communities are informal—this was the inspiration—and in a communal effort, together with the people, you can almost work like in an orchestra, where you have a hundred instruments playing together to create a symphony.

DU: So we want to thank everybody who wanted to become part of this dream and supported us along the way, and we are looking at continuing.

JK: Yeah. And so one day pretty soon, when the colors start going up on these walls, we hope more people will join us, and, you know, join this big dream, and so that maybe one day, the whole of Vila Cruzeiro will be painted.

DU: Thank you.

(Applause)

Unit 6 Melissa Marshall: Talk nerdy to me

Part 1

Five years ago, I experienced a bit of what it must have been like to be Alice in Wonderland. Penn State asked me, a communications teacher, to teach a communications class for engineering students. And I was scared. (Laughter) Really scared. Scared of these students with their big brains and their big books and their big, unfamiliar words. But as these conversations unfolded, I experienced what Alice must have when she went down that rabbit hole and saw that door to a whole new world. That's just how I felt as I had those conversations with the students. I was amazed at the ideas that they had, and I wanted others to experience this wonderland as well. And I believe the key to opening that door is great communication.

We desperately need great communication from our scientists and engineers in order to change the world. Our scientists and engineers are the ones that are tackling our grandest challenges, from energy to environment to health care, among others, and if we don't know about it and understand it, then the work isn't done, and I believe it's our responsibility as non-scientists to have these interactions. But these great conversations can't occur if our scientists and engineers don't invite us in to see their wonderland. So scientists and engineers, please, talk nerdy to us.

Part 2

I want to share a few keys on how you can do that to make sure that we can see that your science is sexy and that your engineering is engaging. First question to answer for us: so what? Tell us why your science is relevant to us. Don't just tell me that you study trabeculae, but tell me that you study trabeculae, which is the mesh-like structure of our bones because it's important to understanding and treating osteoporosis.

And when you're describing your science, beware of jargon. Jargon is a barrier to our understanding of your ideas. Sure, you can say "spatial and temporal," but why not just say "space and time," which is so much more accessible to us? And making your ideas accessible is not the same as dumbing it down. Instead, as Einstein said, make everything as simple as possible, but no simpler. You can clearly communicate your science without compromising the ideas. A few things to consider are having examples, stories, and analogies. Those are ways to engage and excite us about your content. And when presenting your work, drop the bullet points. Have you ever wondered why they're called bullet points? (Laughter) What do bullets do? Bullets kill, and they will kill your presentation. A slide like this is not only boring, but it relies too much on the language area of our brain, and causes us to become overwhelmed. Instead, this example slide by Genevieve Brown is much more effective. It's showing that the special structure of trabeculae are so strong that they actually inspired the unique design of the Eiffel Tower. And the trick here is to use a single, readable sentence that the audience can key into if they get a bit lost, and then provide visuals which appeal to our other senses and create a deeper sense of understanding of what's being described.

Part 3

So I think these are just a few keys that can help the rest of us to open that door and see the wonderland that is science and engineering. And because the engineers that I've worked with have taught me to become really in touch with my inner nerd, I want to summarize with an equation. (Laughter) Take your science, subtract your bullet points and your jargon, divide by relevance, meaning share what's relevant to the audience, and multiply it by the passion that you have for this incredible work that you're doing, and that is going to equal incredible interactions that are full of understanding. And so, scientists and engineers, when you've solved this equation, by all means, talk nerdy to me. (Laughter) Thank you. (Applause)

Grammar Summary

UNIT 1: Present and past tenses

Simple present

I teach children to draw.
She volunteers once a month.
He watches the news on TV every evening.

I don't like to waste food.
You don't often take care of the children.
She doesn't work on Sundays.
They don't help out much.

Do you donate to charity?
Do you recycle waste?
Does he know any volunteers?
Does this charity have branches overseas?

Where do the volunteers go after the event?
Who helps out at the organization?

How often do you volunteer?
How do they reduce the amount of trash?

We use the simple present to talk about:

- things that are always or generally true
  I'm a nurse. I take care of sick people.
- repeated actions and routines
  I take my children to school and then go to the hospital.
- permanent situations
  She works as a doctor in a large hospital.

To form negative sentences and questions in the simple present, we use *do/don't/does/doesn't* with the main verb.

Wh- questions start with a question word (*What*, *Where*, *Who*, *When*, *Why*, *How*, etc.).

Present progressive

I'm waiting for a bus.
You're listening to a podcast about global warming.

I'm not working on any projects currently.
He isn't volunteering this month.

Are we helping to reduce waste?
Is she donating her old furniture?

We use the present progressive to describe:

- events that are happening now or around now
  John is waiting for you in the lobby.
- temporary situations
  We're staying with a friend while we're visiting the city.
- trends
  The amount of trash is increasing every year.

Simple past

She lived in Los Angeles when she was in college.
They started a new company a couple of months ago.

I worked in Seoul last year.
I learned a lot about ways to reduce pollution at the workshop last week.

I didn't know so much food was wasted.
Did you see the presentation on solar energy?

- We use the simple past to talk about completed actions and events in the past. We often include a time phrase (*yesterday*, *last year*, etc.).
- To form negative sentences and questions in the simple past, we use *did/didn't* + the main verb.

Past progressive The doctor was examining the patient. We were studying ways to help the environment. He wasn't working last weekend. They weren't studying when I arrived. Were you helping out this morning? Were they volunteering last Sunday?	We use the past progressive to: • talk about something that continued before and after another action *I was watching TV when she called.* • show that something continued for some time *I was living in Los Angeles.* • talk about past trends *The number of volunteers was increasing.*
Present perfect Cell phones have changed how we keep in touch. He has spent the past two days collecting trash for recycling. They haven't met the other volunteers yet. She hasn't worked for a charity before. Have you ever done any volunteer work? Has he received the letter we sent?	We use the present perfect to: • talk about experiences or things that happened at an unspecified time in the past *He has been to many countries.* • show that something is important in the present *The Internet has made a huge difference in how we get information.* • show that something continues up to the present *They have lived in Tokyo for nine years.*

UNIT 2: *Will* and *going to*

Robots will become very popular. Virtual reality will be the next big thing. There won't be many people without a smartphone in ten years. We probably won't ever use teleportation to travel. Will there be people living on Mars by 2030? Will the Internet of Things really benefit us? I'm certain she is going to be world-famous. We are all going to use technology more. Machines are never going to be as creative as us. I'm sure humans are not going to find aliens. Are robot police going to become common? Is the Internet of Things going to change the way we use our devices?	• We use *will* to make predictions about the future that we are certain about. *I'm sure machines will replace people in most jobs.* • We form negative sentences with *won't* (= *will not*). *There won't be many people without access to the Internet in a few years.* • We can also use *going to* to make predictions about the future. The meaning in most cases is the same as using *will* or *won't*. *Connected devices are going to be everywhere in a few years.*

UNIT 3: Cause and effect

Introduce an effect
Diabetes is a preventable disease, so it's important to have a healthy lifestyle to avoid it.

Introduce a cause
A lot of people use health and fitness wearables because they want to monitor their activity.
Many governments are spending more on health care due to aging populations.
You should exercise for at least 150 minutes a week as it has multiple health benefits.
As a result of early treatment, the patient made a full recovery.
Because of improvements in medical technology, cancer survival rates have increased.

We use the words *so*, *because*, *due to*, *as*, *as a result of*, and *because of* to link two parts of a sentence. All these words except *so* introduce a cause.

Other common linking words are *owing to* and *since*. They both introduce a cause.

- *Owing to* has a similar meaning to *due to*, *as a result of*, and *because of*.
  Owing to the heavy traffic, the doctor was late.
- *Since* has a similar meaning to *because*.
  He was told by his doctor to cut down on red meat, since too much of it can lead to heart disease.

UNIT 4: Making comparisons

Smartphones are easier to use than computers.
The headset was better than we expected.
It's a cheaper product than the one we saw in the other store.

Modern computers are much faster than ones from ten years ago.

This was the most popular app last month.

The new TV we bought is as big as our old one.

This website is not as well-designed as ours.

She has the same smartphone as me.

The way we use technology today is very different from how we used it 15 years ago.

This tablet is the least expensive, but it's also less user-friendly than the other ones.
The design of this smartphone looks the least attractive to me.

- We use the comparative form to compare two things.
- We can add the intensifier *much* to strengthen the comparison.
- We use the superlative form to compare three or more things.
- We use *as* + adjective + *as* to compare two things and say they are the same or equal.
- We use *not as* + adjective + *as* to compare two things and say that one is less than the other.
- We also use *the same … as* and *different from / than* to compare things.
- We can also use *less … than* and *the least* with an adjective.

Regular adjectives

Adjective	Comparative	Superlative
cheap	cheaper	the cheapest
big	bigger	the biggest
simple	simpler	the simplest
healthy	healthier	the healthiest
expensive	more expensive	the most expensive
important	more important	the most important

Irregular adjectives

Adjective	Comparative	Superlative
good	better	the best
bad	worse	the worst
many	more	the most
little	less	the least

UNIT 5: The passive

The river was cleaned up last year.
The river wasn't cleaned up last year.

New facilities were built for the local residents.
New facilities weren't built for the local residents.

The lives of many people were improved by social entrepreneurs.
Students from rural areas were recruited by the college.

Was the project stopped due to lack of money?

Were the houses painted by the villagers?

- We use the passive when we want to focus on an action or the object of the action, rather than on the person who is doing the action.
- We often use the passive because we don't know who or what did the action, or when it isn't important to know. If we want to say who does or did the action (the agent), we use the passive verb + *by* agent.
- We form the simple past passive with the simple past of the verb *be* (*was/were*) + past participle.

We use the simple past passive:

- to talk about past facts
  Barefoot College was founded by Sanjit Roy.
- to describe a past process or series of events
  The corporation was set up, plans were developed, and a new transport system was constructed.

UNIT 6: Verb patterns with *-ing* and infinitive

He dislikes receiving calls late at night.
The presenter recommended not using social media so much.

They decided to create a new social media company.
I intend to send a card to congratulate him on getting engaged.

She hates to lose / hates losing.
He prefers to communicate / prefers communicating by email.

- We use the verb + *-ing* pattern with some verbs, which are never followed by the infinitive. The negative form of this pattern is *not* + *-ing*.
  She usually avoids texting her boss.
  I regret not writing to them.
- We use verb + infinitive with some verbs, which are never followed by *-ing*.
  We agreed to keep in touch via email.
- Some verbs can follow either pattern without changing the basic meaning.
  I love to check / love checking my social media accounts.

She stopped to call her friend. (= She stopped what she was doing and called her friend.)
She stopped chatting with her friend. (= She was chatting with her friend and then she stopped.)

He remembered to go see his sister yesterday. (= This was an action that he needed to do.)

They remembered going on their first vacation together. (= This was a past experience that they remembered.)

The Internet allows us all to keep in touch easily.
He taught his grandmother how to take videos.
Should we invite Jing to take part in the webinar?

- Some verbs can follow either pattern, but there is a change in meaning of the sentence.
I forgot to buy the books for her. (= I didn't buy the books for her because I forgot.)
I won't forget buying my first smartphone. (= I bought a smartphone and the experience is something that I will not forget.)
- We use verb + object + infinitive with some verbs.
She persuaded me to sign up for a new social media account.

verb + *-ing*	**verb + infinitive**	**verb + *-ing* / verb + infinitive with similar meanings**	**verb + object + infinitive**
avoid	agree	begin	allow
consider	aim	continue	ask
dislike	arrange	hate	encourage
enjoy	choose	like	expect
finish	decide	love	force
imagine	expect	prefer	help
keep	hope	start	like
mind	intend		invite
practice	learn	**verb + *-ing* / verb + infinitive with different meanings**	need
recommend	manage		persuade
regret	need		remind
risk	plan	forget	teach
suggest	prepare	remember	tell
	promise	stop	want
	want		would

Acknowledgements

The Author and Publisher would like to thank the following teaching professionals for their valuable input during the development of this series:

Coleeta Paradise Abdullah, Certified Training Center; **Tara Amelia Arntsen**, Northern State University; **Estela Campos**; **Federica Castro**, Pontificia Universidad Católica Madre y Maestra; **Amy Cook**, Bowling Green State University; **Carrie Cheng**, School of Continuing and Professional Studies, the University of Hong Kong; **Mei-ho Chiu**, Soochow University; **Anthony Sean D'Amico**, SDH Institute; **Wilder Yesid Escobar Almeciga**, Universidad El Bosque; **Rosa E. Vasquez Fernandez**, English for International Communication; **Touria Ghaffari**, The Beekman School; **Rosario Giraldez**, Alianza Cultural Uruguay Estados Unidos; **William Haselton**, NC State University; **Yu Huichun**, Macau University of Science and Technology; **Michelle Kim**, TOPIA Education; **Jay Klaphake**, Kyoto University of Foreign Studies; **Kazuteru Kuramoto**, Keio Senior High School; **Michael McCollister**, Feng Chia University; **Jennifer Meldrum**, EC English Language Centers; **Holly Milkowart**, Johnson County Community College; **Nicholas Millward**, Australian Centre for Education; **Stella Maris Palavecino**, Buenos Aires English House; **Youngsun Park**, YBM; **Adam Parmentier**, Mingdao High School; **Jennie Popp**, Universidad Andrés Bello; **Terri Rapoport**, ELS Educational Services; **Erich Rose**, Auburn University; **Yoko Sakurai**, Aichi University; **Mark D. Sheehan**, Hannan University; **DongJin Shin**, Hankuk University of Foreign Studies; **Shizuka Tabara**, Kobe University; **Jeffrey Taschner**, AUA Language Center; **Hadrien Tournier**, Berlitz Corporation; **Rosa Vasquez**, JFK Institute; **Jindarat De Vleeschauwer**, Chiang Mai University; **Tamami Wada**, Chubu University; **Colin Walker**, Myongii University; **Elizabeth Yoon**, Hanyang University; **Keiko Yoshida**, Konan University

And special thanks to: **Peter Draw, Tara Hirebet, Kate Chong, Carrie Cousins, Martín Andrade, Neil Anderson, Janice Reis Lodge, Charles Browne, Craig Albrightson, Priscilla Shunmugam, Mary Kadera**

Credits

Photo Credits

Cover Gerd Ludwig/National Geographic Creative, **3** Kevork Djansezian/Getty Images News/Getty Images, **4** (tl) (tr) © James Duncan Davidson/TED, (cl) © Ryan Lash/TED, (cr) (bl) (br) © James Duncan Davidson/TED, **5** (tl) (tr) © James Duncan Davidson/TED, (cl) © TED, (cr) © Marla Aufmuth/TED, (bl) © Robert Leslie/TED, (br) © Michael Brands/2010 TED Conferences, **6** (tl1) Roslan Rahman/AFP/Getty Images, (tl2) Kazuhiro Nogi/AFP/Getty Images, (cl1) Guido Mieth/Taxi/Getty Images, (cl2) AP Images/Eric Risberg, (bl1) Frances Roberts/Alamy Stock Photo (bl2) © Adelina Iliev, **10–11** © Ryan Lash/TED, **12** © Michael Brands/TED, **13** © James Duncan Davidson/TED, **14** Roslan Rahman/AFP/Getty Images, **15** Courtesy of Peter Draw, **17** © Blare Gooch, **18–19** © Cathy Lee, **21** © James Duncan Davidson/TED, **22** © Gabrielle Plucknette, **24** Jonas Gratzer/LightRocket/Getty Images, **25** © James Duncan Davidson/TED, **26** Kazuhiro Nogi/AFP/Getty Images, **27** © Daylon Soh, **29** Javier Larrea/Age Footstock/Getty Images, **30–31** © YouTube, **33** © James Duncan Davidson/TED, **34** © TED, **35** © James Duncan Davidson/TED, **36** Justin Sullivan/Getty Images, **37** © Ryan Lash/TED, **38** Guido Mieth/Taxi/Getty Images, **39** © Kate Chong, **41** Aung Naing Soe/Anadolu Agency/Getty Images, **43** Stephane De Sakutin/AFP/Getty Images, **45** © Ryan Lash/TED, **46** © TED, **47** © Ryan Lash/TED, **48** Jean-Francois Monier/AFP/Getty Images, **49** © Cengage Learning, **51** © James Duncan Davidson/TED, **52** Iryna Denysova/Shutterstock.com, **53** Courtesy of Carrie Cousins, **55** Scott Eells/Bloomberg/Getty Images, **56–57** AP Images/Eric Risberg, **59** © James Duncan Davidson/TED, **60** Carl De Souza/AFP/Getty Images, **61** © James Duncan Davidson/TED, **62** David Ramos/Stringer/Getty Images News/Getty Images, **63** © James Duncan Davidson/TED, **64** Frances Roberts/Alamy Stock Photo, **65** Courtesy of Martín Andrade, **66** (l) De Agostini/Getty Images, (r) Laurie Noble/Photolibrary/Getty Images, **67** Loop Images/UIG/Getty Images, **68–69** © Dieter Telemans/Panos Pictures, **71** © James Duncan Davidson/TED, **73** Andrea Pistolesi/Photolibrary/Getty Images, **74** Lisa Maree Williams/Stringer/Getty Images News/Getty Images, **75** © James Duncan Davidson/TED, **76** © Adelina Iliev, **77** Courtesy of Neil Anderson, **79** © Jiangang Wang, **81** © Brian Yen, **83** © James Duncan Davidson/TED, **84** © Malcolm Nason, **85** © James Duncan Davidson/TED, **86** Aksonov/E+/Getty Images, **87** © Cengage Learning, **168** (l) leungchopan/Shutterstock.com, (r) Wayne0216/Shutterstock.com

Illustration & Infographic Credits

16, 28, 40, 54, 66, 78 emc design; **18, 42, 52, 80** MPS North America LLC

Data sources for infographics: **28** Bernard Marr, www.intel.com, **40** getreferralmd.com, mhealthintelligence.com, uk.reuters.com, **54** www.mycustomer.com, **66** melaka-riverwalk.blogspot.sg, www.theantdaily.com, www.wepa-db.net, **78** circle.espire.com/thread/6552

Keynote

3A COMBO SPLIT

Workbook

Ingrid Wisniewska

NATIONAL GEOGRAPHIC LEARNING | CENGAGE Learning

Australia • Brazil • Mexico • Singapore • United Kingdom • United States

Contents

Scope and Sequence

UNIT		LESSON A	LESSON B
TITLE		VOCABULARY LISTENING	LANGUAGE FOCUS LISTENING FOCUS
1	**Making a Difference**	Giving help Inspiring dreams	Discussing ways to contribute Reduced speech
2	**Trends**	Describing trends Analyzing trends	Future trends Intonation
3	**Improving Lives**	Talking about healthcare The health check of the future?	Discussing cause and effect Stress for emphasis
4	**Designing the Web**	Describing website features Designing websites	Making comparisons Linking
5	**Community Builders**	Making communities better Creating green spaces	Using the passive voice Word stress: *can* and *can't*
6	**Clear Communication**	Using communication collocations Communication styles	Describing types of communicators Intonation when agreeing and disagreeing

LESSON C	LESSON D	LESSON E
VOCABULARY BUILDING	**TED PLAYLIST**	**WRITING**
Prefix *min-*	How to step up in the face of disaster Cheap effective shelter for disaster relief Emergency shelters made from paper	Desribing an inspiring person
Collocations with *advantage*	How yarn bombing grew into a worldwide movement The tribes we lead Meet the founder of the blog revolution	Describing a product or service
Collocations with *pressure*	A warm embrace that saves lives Printing a human kidney A test for Parkinson's with a phone call	A letter to a health tech company
Word group *attach*	Human-centered design A delightful way to teach kids about computers Simplicity sells	Writing a review
Suffix *-ant*	Building a park in the sky A park underneath the hustle and bustle of New York City A guerilla gardener in South Central LA	Making a suggestion
Collocations with *span*	CERN's supercollider The most mysterious star in the universe How we'll find life on other planets	Giving an explanation

1 Making a Difference

1A

VOCABULARY Giving help

A Complete the paragraph using the correct form of the words or phrases in the box.

be there for them	encourage	help out
make an impact	take care of	inspiring

My social studies teacher in sixth grade was a very [1] ______________________ person. He made us believe we could make a difference. He told us that even small acts of kindness could [2] ______________________ on the people around us. He [3] ______________________ us to find ways to help people in the community. We could offer to [4] ______________________ around the neighborhood. One way I used to help my neighbors was to [5] ______________________ their pets when they were away. Small acts of kindness like these show others that we will [6] ______________________ if they ever need help.

B Answer the questions using your own words.

1 When was the last time someone helped you out?

____

2 How do you try to make a difference to the people around you?

____

LISTENING Inspiring dreams

A ▶ 1.1 Listen to a podcast. What is it about?

a Three charities you should volunteer to help.

b How to create a volunteer program.

c How to choose the best volunteer program.

B ▶ 1.1 Listen again. Which pieces of advice are mentioned in the talk? Check [✓] all that apply.

1 ☐ give volunteers paid time off

2 ☐ create volunteer teams

3 ☐ make a list of charities that need help

4 ☐ force employees to volunteer

5 ☐ show appreciation to volunteers

COMMUNICATION Talking about helping others

A Circle the best response for each question.

1 Do your classmates often ask you for help?

a Yeah, sometimes. I help them with their homework.

b Thanks, I can manage on my own.

2 Have you helped any of your neighbors recently?

a No way! As much as possible, I try not to ask anyone for help.

b Well, I watered Mrs. Green's plants while she was on vacation last week.

3 When was the last time you helped a stranger?

a Um, I guess it was a couple of weeks ago.

b Sure. What's the problem?

B Answer the questions using your own words.

1 When was the last time you helped someone out?

____

2 What did you do for them?

____

3 How did they feel about it?

____

1B

LANGUAGE FOCUS Discussing ways to contribute

A Complete the conversation. Number the sentences (**1–8**) in the correct order.

a ______ Sounds like you had a good time. Maybe I should volunteer too.

b __5__ Wow! That must have been really hard work.

c __1__ Have you volunteered before?

d ______ Well, I worked with other volunteers and we painted all the children's rooms.

e ______ What did you do there?

f ______ I guess it was. But I enjoyed it a lot and the kids were really happy.

g ______ Yes, I have. I helped out an orphanage once.

h ______ You should. It can be a lot of fun, and it's a chance to make a difference.

B Circle the correct word to complete each sentence.

1 Did you (**volunteer** / **volunteered**) last year?

2 I've (**signed** / **sign**) up as a volunteer at the animal shelter.

3 How do you (**helped** / **help**) other people in your daily life?

4 Volunteering (**has changed** / **was changing**) my outlook on life. I am now more grateful for all I have.

5 I developed an app to help abuse victims when I (**was working** / **am working**) at the children's home.

C Find and correct the three mistakes in the paragraph below.

I often volunteer to help out at charity fund-raisers. I've been to three events last year, and I've been to two so far this year. The last event I went to was for a children's charity. In total, the event was raising over $100,000! It's so nice to feel that I played a part in that. I also get to meet a lot of new people, and I've made so many new friends. I even meet my husband at a charity event three years ago.

LISTENING FOCUS Reduced speech

A ▶ **1.2** We often make words and phrases shorter when we speak. This is called reduced speech. Listen to and repeat the examples.

What **do you** do as a volunteer? → **Whaddaya** do as a volunteer?

What **did you** do as a volunteer? → **Whadidja** do as a volunteer?

B ▶ **1.3** Listen to each question. Circle the word you hear.

1 What kind of work (**do** / **did**) you do?

2 How (**do** / **did**) you get to work?

3 Who (**do** / **did**) you ask for help?

4 What (**do** / **did**) you like about being a volunteer?

C ▶ **1.4** Listen to each question. Circle the best response.

1 **a** I work in an orphanage.

b I worked in an orphanage.

2 **a** Yes, I really enjoyed working there.

b Yes, I really enjoy working there.

3 **a** I help them with their studies.

b I helped them with their studies.

4 **a** Yes, I do.

b Yes, I did.

1C

READING

Read the passage and answer the questions.

As a 14-year-old, Australian Hugh Evans joined a volunteer program and traveled to some of the poorest parts of Manila in the Philippines. The experience made such an impact on him that he decided to devote his life to ending extreme poverty.

Hugh Evans (left) speaks at the Global Citizen Festival, New York.

Evans's goal is to make a difference in the world. As a college student, he started the Oaktree Foundation, which raised millions of dollars for schools and education programs in developing countries. After that, he led a campaign to persuade the Australian government to double its foreign aid. The campaign organized a huge concert—the *Make Poverty History* concert. The aim of the free concert was not to raise money but to raise awareness of world poverty and to persuade world financial leaders to increase aid to developing countries.

Evans continues to be passionate about raising awareness of world poverty—now using the power of the Internet. In 2008, he founded the Global Poverty Project to campaign for government and business leaders to take more action against poverty. The organization engages and educates people about world poverty through an online community of volunteers, and is committed to ending world poverty by 2020.

In 2011, the Global Poverty Project organized the Global Citizen Festival in Central Park in New York City. To get tickets, people had to sign up on the website and get points by taking actions toward ending world poverty (for example, by watching a video, signing an online petition, writing a letter, or donating money to a charity).

Sixty thousand people attended the festival and helped to raise $1.3 billion for projects to fight poverty. The festival inspired thousands of people to help end world poverty. Every person in the audience was committed to making a difference. And that is the start of long-term sustainable change.

A What is the passage mainly about? Circle the best answer.

a a man who donated a huge amount of money to charity

b a man who spent his life as a volunteer in poor countries

c a man who engaged people to take action against poverty

B Circle **T** for true, **F** for false, or **NG** for not given.

1	Hugh Evans was inspired by a visit to the Philippines.	**T**	**F**	**NG**
2	Evans worked as a volunteer at a school in Manila.	**T**	**F**	**NG**
3	Evans was a student when he founded the Oaktree Foundation.	**T**	**F**	**NG**
4	The main aim of the Make Poverty History concert was to raise money.	**T**	**F**	**NG**
5	There was no admission fee for the Make Poverty History concert.	**T**	**F**	**NG**
6	The Global Citizen Festival raised $1.3 billion.	**T**	**F**	**NG**

LISTENING

A ▶ **1.5** Listen. What is the talk mainly about?

a the problems faced by charities in developing countries

b one charity that provides sustainable help to poor communities

c charities that help poor communities in developing countries

B ▶ **1.5** Listen again. What kind of aid does this charity give? Check [✓] all that are mentioned in the talk.

1 money ☐ **2** food ☐ **3** water ☐ **4** animals ☐ **5** training ☐

C **CRITICAL THINKING** Use the information (**a–e**) to complete the Venn diagram. Look back at the reading on page 9 if necessary.

a founded in the 21st century

b aims to convince world leaders to take action to end poverty

c focuses on long-term sustainable change

d founded by a farmer

e works actively to educate people

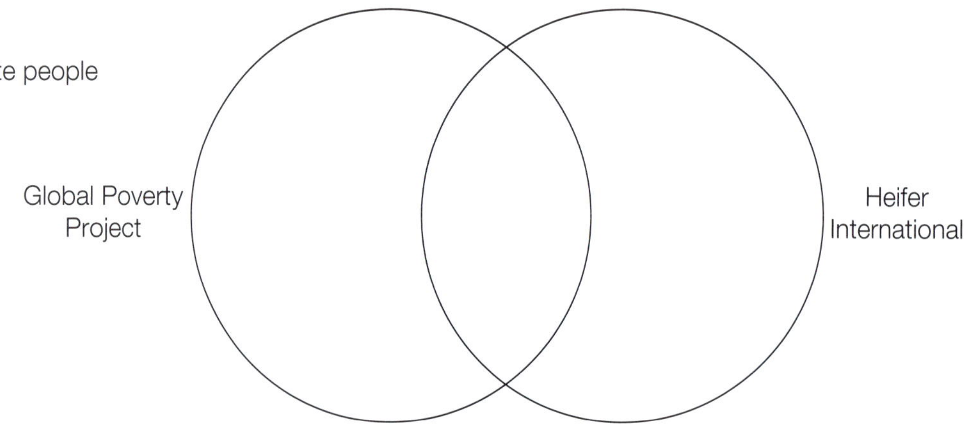

VOCABULARY BUILDING

A Choose a word from the box to replace each word in **bold**.

committed	devote	insignificant
minimize	passionate	

1 Small actions can seem **unimportant** but they can have a big impact. ______________

2 Many people are **very enthusiastic** about making a difference. ______________

3 Some people are **determined** to help end poverty. ______________

4 It's a good idea to **reduce** the amount of energy we use. ______________

5 It's inspiring to see people who **completely give** their lives to helping others. ______________

B The prefix *min-* means *small* or *less*, for example *minimize*. Match the words to the correct definition.

1 minimum (*n.*)	○	○	**a** lesser or secondary in importance
2 miniature (*adj.*)	○	○	**b** the least possible amount of something
3 minor (*adj.*)	○	○	**c** smaller than others of the same kind

C Complete the sentences using the words in the box.

miniature	minimum	minor

1 She had a very ______________________________ role in the play.

2 The ______________________________ sum to donate is ten dollars.

3 The toy house was filled with ______________________________ chairs and tables.

Aid is delivered in Aceh after the Indian Ocean Earthquake and Tsunami in 2004.

TEDTALKS

1D

TED PLAYLIST

Residents of Fukuchiyama, Japan, are rescued from severe flooding.

HOW TO STEP UP IN THE FACE OF DISASTER

When a tornado hit their hometown in the United States, sisters Caitria and Morgan O'Neill—just 20 and 24 at the time—realized there was a desperate need for someone with the skills to organize people and the supplies to help. So they took charge and are now teaching others how to do the same with their website Recovers.org.

CHEAP, EFFECTIVE SHELTER FOR DISASTER RELIEF

After a disaster, people need shelter immediately, but it takes a long time to build temporary housing. Michael McDaniel designed housing that is inexpensive, easy to transport, and easy to set up. But he couldn't find anyone to build it. In the end, he decided to start his own company. In this talk, he shows us his Exo Reaction Housing Solution.

EMERGENCY SHELTERS MADE FROM PAPER

Imagine a house made from cardboard paper tubes. Prize-winning architect Shigeru Ban has designed museums and other important buildings. But he wanted to use architecture to help ordinary people. So he started building houses from materials such as cardboard tubes for people affected by natural disasters.

A What is each talk about? Match the topic to the speaker.

1 buildings made from simple materials ○ ○ **a** Caitria and Morgan O'Neill
2 organizing help after a disaster ○ ○ **b** Michael McDaniel
3 quick and easy homes for the homeless ○ ○ **c** Shigeru Ban

B Which speakers most likely said the following? Circle the correct answer.

1 "We spent five weeks rebuilding the church. It was meant to stay there for three years, but actually it stayed there 10 years."
   a Caitria and Morgan O'Neill **b** Michael McDaniel **c** Shigeru Ban
2 "We just started answering questions and making decisions because someone—anyone—had to. And why not me?"
   a Caitria and Morgan O'Neill **b** Michael McDaniel **c** Shigeru Ban
3 "They can actually stack together so we get extremely efficient transportation and storage out of them."
   a Caitria and Morgan O'Neill **b** Michael McDaniel **c** Shigeru Ban

C Decide which talk you most want to watch. Watch it online at www.ted.com.

1E

WRITING Describing an inspiring person

A Read the sample paragraph about a person who's made an impact on someone's life.

Write one paragraph. Start by describing someone who inspired you.

Use some new words from this unit.

Someone who has made a big difference in my life is my English teacher in high school. She was very sensitive and kind. I didn't like school very much because I didn't have any friends. I think she noticed that I was sad. So she encouraged me to read and gave me a list of books to read during the summer vacation. I learned to love reading, a habit that has stayed with me all my life. Now I am in college studying English literature! I haven't forgotten my high school teacher, and whenever I have time, I volunteer at our local public library to read stories with children. I hope to help them learn to love reading, too.

Then say how you felt before they helped you.

Describe how they inspired you.

Say how this has changed your life.

B Think about someone you know who has made a difference in your life. Answer the questions to plan your paragraph.

1 Who was the person who inspired you? What was special about them?

2 How did you feel before they helped you?

3 What did they inspire you to do?

4 What kind of impact has this had on your life?

C Now write your paragraph. Then complete the checklist below.

- ☐ Did you use correct spelling and punctuation?
- ☐ Did you use verb tenses correctly?
- ☐ Did you use some new words from this unit?
- ☐ Did you give an example of how your life has changed?

2 Trends

2A

VOCABULARY Describing trends

A Complete the information. Circle the correct words.

In recent years, improvements in technology have led to [1] (**growing** / **more and more**) jobs being carried out by machines rather than humans. According to a Pew Research report, almost half of all current jobs in the United States could disappear by 2025 as a result of [2] (**widespread** / **shrinking**) automation.

Travel agencies, for example, have [3] (**decreased** / **gotten worse**) in number as more and more people choose to book their vacations online. When you go to a bank, it is now quite [4] (**common** / **increasing**) to carry out your transactions through a machine rather than interacting with a human.

Are any jobs still safe? Experts suggest that jobs requiring creativity and social skills are the safest. The number of hairdressers and beauty salons, for example, is still [5] (**growing** / **more and more**).

B Answer the questions using your own words.

1 In the future, do you think the number of jobs done by machines will **increase**? Why or why not?

____

____

2 Do you think robot teachers will ever become **common**? Why or why not?

____

____

3 Do you think society will **improve** if more jobs are done by machines? Why or why not?

____

____

LISTENING Analyzing trends

A ▶ 2.1 Listen. Circle the correct answer.

1 What is the talk mainly about?

a why blogs are popular **b** the history of blogs

2 According to the talk, which of the following is true about blogs?

a They are still popular today. **b** They are starting to become less popular.

B ▶ **2.1** Listen again. Circle **T** for true, **F** for false, or **NG** for not given.

1	Blogging became popular in the early 1990s.	**T**	**F**	**NG**
2	The word *blog* was first used in the 1990s.	**T**	**F**	**NG**
3	The word *blog* is a short form of the word *blogger*.	**T**	**F**	**NG**
4	Music blogs are more common than technology blogs.	**T**	**F**	**NG**
5	Big companies spend millions of dollars developing blogs.	**T**	**F**	**NG**
6	Today, there are around 150 million blogs on the Internet.	**T**	**F**	**NG**

COMMUNICATION Talking about trends

A Complete the conversation. Number the sentences (**1–6**) in the correct order.

a ______ Well, I use an app that gives me recommendations.
b ______ I agree. How do you decide which movies to watch? There are so many online.
c __1__ Do you prefer watching movies online or buying DVDs?
d ______ Good idea! How about movie blogs, do you read those too?
e ______ That's easy, definitely online. DVDs take up too much space.
f ______ Oh, yes! I follow several blogs to find out about new movies.

B Answer the questions using your own words.

1 Do you prefer watching movies online or buying DVDs? Why?

____

____

2 How do you decide what movies to watch or what music to listen to?

____

____

2B

LANGUAGE FOCUS Future trends

A Circle the best option to complete each sentence.

1 In fifty years, there (**will** / **won't**) be printed textbooks in the classroom. Students will all have tablets.

2 Robots (**will** / **won't**) be a common household item. Everyone will have one.

3 People (**are** / **aren't**) going to be more connected to the Internet. Everything we own will be linked to it.

4 Shopping online (**is** / **isn't**) going to be the most popular way to shop. There will be fewer stores.

B Circle the best response.

1 I'm going to go for a jog this evening.
  a I'm sorry I couldn't come along.
  b That's great! Can I join you?
2 I don't think I'll be able to join you for dinner.
  a Oh no, shall we meet another time?
  b It's OK. We had a great time.
3 I think home robots will become very popular in the next five years.
  a I don't think it will be so soon.
  b It was a great invention that benefited mankind.
4 Are you going to Maria's birthday party?
  a No, I couldn't make it.
  b Yes. I'm bringing my cousin, too.

C Make predictions about the future using the words provided and *will* or *going to*.

1 artificial intelligence / become / more widespread / five years

____

2 humans / live / on other planets / 20 years from now

____

3 time travel / not be possible / in ten years time

____

4 cars and trains / not change very much / in the next five years

____

LISTENING FOCUS Intonation

A ▶ 2.2 We use intonation to stress words that contrast with each other. Notice how the speaker's voice rises on the first choice and falls on the second. Listen and repeat what you hear.

Do you think life in the future will be **better**, or **worse**?

Do you think robots will make life **easier**, or more **difficult**?

B ▶ 2.3 Read the questions. Underline the words that should be stressed. Then listen to check your answers.

1 Do you think people will have more free time, or less?
2 Will cities become larger, or smaller?
3 Do you think air travel will be faster, or just the same?
4 Will the world's population increase, or decrease?

C ▶ 2.3 Listen again. Draw arrows to show the intonation.

2C

READING

Read the passage and answer the questions.

1 Do you think you know a lot about the latest trends in fashion, music, and culture? Then you might be the right person for a job as a coolhunter!

2 In today's interconnected world, trends spread, and change, quicker than ever before. What's in fashion one week can become outdated the next. It's therefore vital for many companies to keep up to date with what's trending and make sure their products stay popular. This is where coolhunters earn their dollars.

3 A coolhunter's job is it to spot patterns and make predictions about what will become the next big thing. Most coolhunters work in the fields of fashion, design, or technology. Many of them also have their own blogs, where they identify current trends and post pictures of the latest fashion and design ideas.

4 But how does a coolhunter stay ahead of the game? Networking is important. Many coolhunters have a network of social, business, and online contacts. These could be influential bloggers or other trendsetters, such as magazine editors or key decision makers in other companies.

5 It's also important for coolhunters to observe the people around them. They need to take notice of people's clothing, accessories, and gadgets. They often spend time socializing, and are constantly looking for the coolest new places to hang out.

Aimee Song is a popular fashion and interior design blogger.

6 And of course, being active online is vital for any modern coolhunter. Spending time online, visiting websites, writing blogs, and engaging in social media networks are the most effective ways of finding out what's hot and what's not.

7 The number of people employed as coolhunters is expected to rise in the future. There are even universities that offer coolhunting courses. So if you're hunting for a cool new career, perhaps this is the one for you!

A Match the headings with the paragraphs.

1 People Watching	○	○	**a** Paragraph 3
2 Networking	○	○	**b** Paragraph 4
3 Having an Online Presence	○	○	**c** Paragraph 5
4 What is a Coolhunter?	○	○	**d** Paragraph 6

B Circle the best answers according to the information in the passage.

1 How are trends different nowadays?

a They change more rapidly. **b** They are started by younger people.

2 Which of these would be a good contact for a coolhunter?

a A famous sports person **b** The CEO of a technology company

3 How is the number of coolhunter jobs expected to change in the future?

a It's likely to rise. **b** It's likely to fall.

LISTENING

A ▶ **2.4** Listen. Check [✓] the influences on fashion trends that are mentioned in the talk.

☐ street styles ☐ famous designers ☐ friends

☐ fashion shows ☐ fashion bloggers ☐ celebrities

B ▶ **2.4** Listen again. Circle the best answers according to the information in the talk.

1 What is street style?

a fashion worn by ordinary people **b** the latest fashion for casual wear

2 Why is the fashion blogger Chiara Ferragni mentioned?

a because she made a lot of money from her fashion blog
b because she has a huge number of online followers

3 Why are some people becoming increasingly influenced by their friends' fashion ideas?

a because social media makes it easier to share pictures of fashion styles
b because our friends' opinions are becoming more important to us

4 What does the speaker say about trendsetters?

a There are fewer trendsetters than ever before.
b Due to social media, more people have the opportunity to be a trendsetter.

C **CRITICAL THINKING** Who do you think has a greater influence on trends: coolhunters or fashion bloggers? Give a reason to support your answer.

____

____

VOCABULARY BUILDING

A Complete the paragraph using the correct form of the words in the box.

analyze	emerge	relevant	take advantage of

Companies nowadays are [1] ________________ online resources to find out more about their customers. They have found that social media tools are becoming far more [2] ________________ to customer choices. For example, researchers who [3] ________________ a group of parents found that the majority of them regularly consulted social media sites before making purchases for their children. As a result, a new market is [4] ________________ for social media marketing experts.

B Read the paragraph below. Then choose the correct word to complete each sentence.

The Internet has changed customer shopping habits. Customers can now **take advantage of** the latest sales and promotions that are posted through websites, emails, online ads, and social media sites. Some businesses offer their customers the added convenience of shopping from the comfort of their own homes. This might seem like an **unfair advantage** over smaller businesses that are unable to offer the same services, but it is what consumers want and prefer—convenience at the click of a mouse. For these smaller businesses, it will definitely be **to their advantage** to harness the power of the Internet to reach more customers.

1 If you take advantage of something, you (**don't use** / **make good use of**) it.

2 If something is to your advantage, it will (**benefit** / **harm**) you.

3 If you have an unfair advantage, it's (**easier** / **harder**) for you to achieve something you would have had to work hard for.

TEDTALKS

2D

TED PLAYLIST

Yarn bombing of a bicycle in Cheshire, United Kingdom

HOW YARN BOMBING GREW INTO A WORLDWIDE MOVEMENT

Textile artist Magda Sayeg transforms urban landscapes into her own playground by decorating everyday objects with colorful knit works. These warm, fuzzy "yarn bombs" started small, but soon people took a liking to the craft and it spread across the world.

THE TRIBES WE LEAD

Seth Godin argues that the Internet has revived a human social unit from the distant past: tribes. He explains that the Internet gives us the power to find people who share the same ideas and values—giving ordinary people the power to lead and make a change. He encourages all of us to take advantage of this and start a tribe.

MEET THE FOUNDER OF THE BLOG REVOLUTION

The founding mother of the blog revolution, Movable Type's Mena Trott, talks about the early days of blogging, when she realized that giving regular people the power to share their lives online is the key to building a friendlier, more connected world.

A What is the theme of the playlist? Circle the best answer.

a new technology **b** trendsetting **c** being a leader

B Which speakers most likely said the following? Match the quote to the speaker.

1 "I reached all of these people, and I had tens of thousands of people reading about my life every day." ○	○	**a** Magda Sayeg
2 "What I want you to do, it only takes 24 hours, is: create a movement." ○	○	**b** Seth Godin
3 "And this was fun for me. It was really fun to take inanimate objects and have them come to life." ○	○	**c** Mena Trott

C Decide which talk you most want to watch. Watch it online at www.ted.com.

2E

WRITING Describing a product or service

A Read the sample passage about a new product.

Write two paragraphs. In the first paragraph, describe your product or service.	Food scanners will become more popular in the future. People are paying more and more attention to what they eat, and this product will be able to instantly analyze the ingredients in food.	Use some new words from this unit.
In the second paragraph, describe the benefits of this product or service.	This will help people make informed decisions about their purchases. It will be especially beneficial for people who suffer from food allergies. Other useful applications of this product could be to analyze how many calories are in the food. This will benefit people who need to reduce their calorie intake or those who want to maintain a healthy diet.	Say who it will be useful for. Describe some other applications.

B Think about an idea for a new product or service. Answer the questions to plan your paragraph.

1 What is the product or service?

2 Who will this product or service be good for?

3 How will people benefit from it?

4 What possible applications could there be?

C Now write your paragraph. Then complete the checklist below.

- ☐ Did you use correct spelling and punctuation?
- ☐ Did you use some new words from this unit?
- ☐ Did you explain how it is used?
- ☐ Did you describe how it will help people?

3 Improving Lives

3A

VOCABULARY Talking about healthcare

A Complete the sentences using the words in the box.

motivate **suffers from** **treatment** **wearable**

1 Smartwatches and fitness trackers are examples of ______________ technology.

2 I joined a support group to ______________ me on my weight loss journey.

3 My brother ______________ depression—there are days when he won't even leave his room.

4 Scientists have come up with a new ______________ for baldness in both men and women.

B Answer the questions using your own words.

1 Do you know someone who is a caregiver? What do they do?

____

2 Do you have any elderly family members? What kinds of healthcare do they receive?

____

3 Do you monitor your health? What do you do?

____

4 If you could find the cure for a disease, which disease would you choose? Why?

____

LISTENING The health check of the future?

A ▶ 3.1 Listen. Circle the best answer.

1 What is the talk about?
   - **a** a new medical robot that has been developed
   - **b** the possibility that robots that will replace human doctors
   - **c** how robot doctors can read patients' emotions

2 This talk discusses robots that can ___.
   - **a** identify health problems
   - **b** perform surgery
   - **c** provide care at home

B ▶ 3.1 Listen again. Complete the table using information from the talk.

Advantages of medical robots	Disadvantages of medical robots
Robots can perform [1] ______________ tests on patients.	Robots do not include [3] ______________ and [4] ______________ factors in their diagnosis.
Doctors can spend more time specializing in illnesses that are more [2] ______________.	Robots can't provide counselling and emotional [5] ______________ to patients.

COMMUNICATION Talking about staying healthy

A Complete the conversation. Number the sentences (**1–6**) in the correct order.

a ______ Thanks! Well, I try to eat a healthy diet and keep active.

b ______ Hmmm... Maybe I'll join you one day.

c ______ Do you do a lot of exercise?

d __1__ Wow! You're looking great! What's your secret?

e ______ Yeah, I go running at least three times a week.

f ______ Sure! It'll be great to exercise together.

B Answer the questions using your own words.

1 How often do you exercise?

____

2 What kind of sport or exercise would you like to do more often?

____

3 How could you make your lifestyle more active?

____

3B

LANGUAGE FOCUS Discussing cause and effect

A Complete the sentences using the words in the box.

result	because	due	so

1 You should brush your teeth every day ______________ you don't get cavities.

2 As a ______________ of having better healthcare for expectant mothers, infant mortality has decreased.

3 Obesity is on the rise ______________ people are eating more junk food.

4 The hospital could not cope with the high volume of patients ______________ to a shortage of doctors.

B Circle the correct words to complete the information.

People now are able to live much longer [1] (**so** / **because of**) improvements in medical care. The rate of deaths [2] (**due to** / **because**) cancer and other illnesses has fallen [3] (**because** / **as a result of**) new drugs and better medical technology. Sadly however, the cost of this medical care makes it difficult for everyone to benefit from it.

In some countries, health insurance is paid for through taxes [4] (**so** / **because**) people don't have to worry about the cost of hospital or doctor visits. However, there are countries where health insurance is private and costs a lot of money. People often delay going to the doctor [5] (**so** / **as**) it is so expensive. In poorer countries, basic healthcare is not even available [6] (**because** / **because of**) there aren't sufficient resources.

C Match the two parts of each sentence.

1 You should cut down your smoking as	○ ○	**a** they keep your heart healthy.
2 Obesity in children is often due to	○ ○	**b** cancer patients are able to live longer.
3 He had a heart attack last year,	○ ○	**c** fast food and a lack of exercise.
4 As a result of new drugs and treatments,	○ ○	**d** it causes many health complications.
5 Healthy fats are good for you because	○ ○	**e** so he's very careful with his diet.

LISTENING FOCUS Stress for emphasis

A ▶ 3.2 We often place extra stress on key words in a conversation. Listen to and repeat the examples.

1 **A:** When do you usually play tennis?
B: I usually play tennis on **Sundays**.

2 **A:** What do you usually do on Sundays?
B: I usually **play tennis** on Sundays.

B ▶ 3.3 Read the examples. Underline one word in the answer to each question that you think should be given extra stress. Listen and check your answers.

1 **A:** When are you having lunch with Daniel?
B: I'm having lunch with him tomorrow.

2 **A:** Who are you having lunch with tomorrow?
B: I'm having lunch with Daniel tomorrow.

3 **A:** Are you having dinner with Daniel tomorrow?
B: No. I'm having lunch with him tomorrow.

C ▶ 3.4 Listen to each question. Circle the best answer.

1 **a** I usually eat **fruit** for breakfast. **b** I usually eat fruit for **breakfast**.

2 **a** I go to the **gym** after work. **b** I go to the gym **after work**.

3 **a** My **father** bought me this watch. **b** My father bought me this **watch**.

4 **a** The **doctor** told me to rest. **b** The doctor told me to **rest**.

3C

READING

Read the passage and answer the questions.

1 Advances in medical technology are helping many people who have Parkinson's disease. While there is still no cure, new innovative devices are improving the quality of life for Parkinson's sufferers.

2 Parkinson's disease affects a person's muscles and their ability to move. It is caused by a problem with the nerve cells in the brain. There is an important chemical called dopamine, which helps send signals to different parts of the brain, telling it when to move parts of the body. However, people with Parkinson's don't produce enough dopamine. As a result, they can't send the correct signals to their arms or legs when they want to move.

3 The main symptom of Parkinson's is constant tremors or shaking of the arms and legs, so patients tend to move very slowly. They have difficulty balancing when they are standing or walking. They may also have trouble speaking and eating. Parkinson's is a progressive disease, which means it gradually gets worse, but this can take a number of years.

4 There are many different kinds of medication to treat Parkinson's. Although some have been successful in slowing down the disease, none are able to completely cure it. One problem that scientists face is monitoring how much medication is needed by each patient. This is where technology is important. New wearable devices detect tremors and classify them based on their intensity. The data is then sent to doctors, allowing them to track patients' reactions to different medication doses.

The devices worn by Parkinson's sufferers are worn on the wrist like a smartwatch.

5 There may be no cure for Parkinson's yet, but with new advancements in drugs and wearable technology, there is hope that patients can have a better quality of life.

A Match each paragraph to its main idea.

1 Paragraph 2 ○ ○ **a** a new way to help people with Parkinson's disease
2 Paragraph 3 ○ ○ **b** how Parkinson's disease affects a person's behavior
3 Paragraph 4 ○ ○ **c** what causes Parkinson's disease

B Circle **T** for true, **F** for false, or **NG** for not given.

1	People who smoke are more likely to get Parkinson's disease.	**T**	**F**	**NG**
2	Parkinson's disease affects the function of the brain.	**T**	**F**	**NG**
3	Parkinson's disease usually develops very rapidly.	**T**	**F**	**NG**
4	Parkinson's disease can affect someone's ability to talk.	**T**	**F**	**NG**
5	Parkinson's disease is becoming more common.	**T**	**F**	**NG**
6	Scientists have discovered a cure for Parkinson's disease.	**T**	**F**	**NG**
7	The device detects a tremor and measures its strength.	**T**	**F**	**NG**

LISTENING

A ▶ **3.5** Listen. What can the device in the talk do?

a prevent heart disease **b** measure weight loss **c** monitor your health

B ▶ **3.5** Listen again. Circle the correct answer.

1 What does this device look like?
a a smartwatch **b** a small bandage

2 What is it used for?
a to collect data from a person's body **b** to treat certain diseases

3 Which of these is true about the device?
a It can collect data from a person's sweat. **b** It can predict when a heart attack will happen.

C **CRITICAL THINKING** Use the information (**a–d**) to complete the Venn diagram. Look back at the reading on page 25 if necessary.

a It is a device you wear on your arm.
b Its sensor can detect shaking.
c Its sensor can detect your blood sugar level.
d It can send data to a doctor.

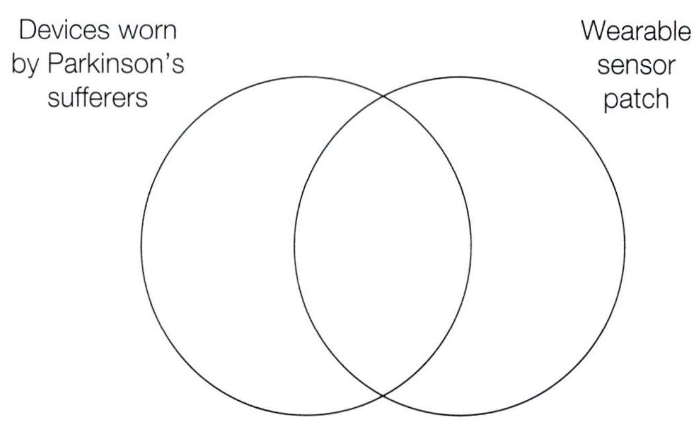

VOCABULARY BUILDING

A Choose a word from the box to replace each word in **bold**.

approach	behavior	constant	pressure	prevent

1 It may be possible to **stop** cancer by analyzing your DNA. ________________

2 Herbal medicine is an alternative healthcare **method**. ________________

3 There is a **never-ending** shortage of doctors and nurses in this hospital. ________________

4 The students were under a lot of **stress** to complete their assignment on time. ________________

5 Doctors monitor the **actions** of their patients to make sure there are no side effects to treatment. ________________

B Complete the sentences with the correct words.

blood pressure: *n.* the amount of force with which blood flows around the body
peer pressure: *n.* the social influence among people of the same group
under pressure: *ph.* to feel a lot of stress from somebody or something

1 He was ________________ to pass his final medical paper.

2 People with high ________________ are at risk of heart diseases.

3 Teenagers face a lot of ________________ from their schoolmates.

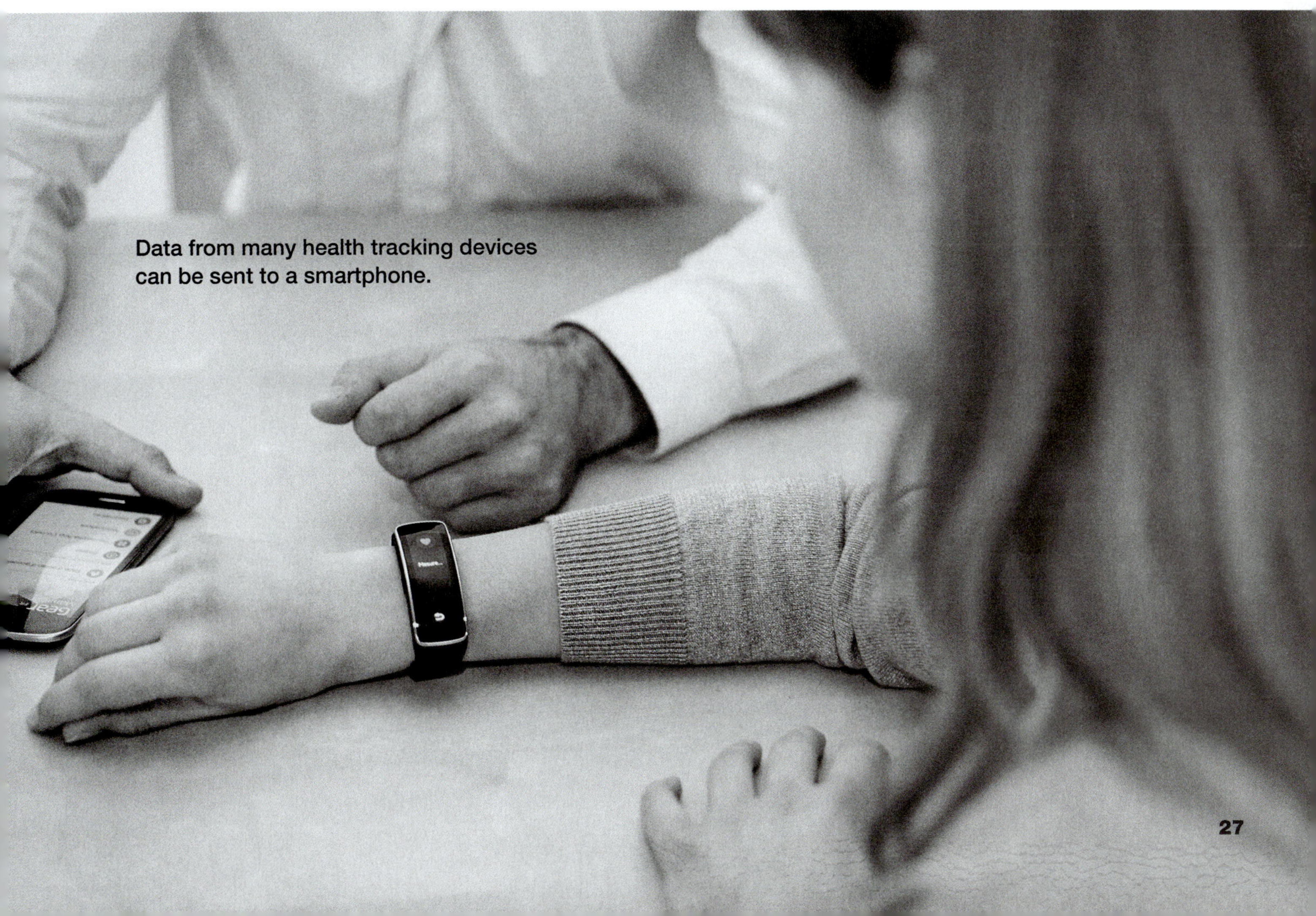

Data from many health tracking devices can be sent to a smartphone.

3D

TED PLAYLIST

A doctor holds up 3D-printed model hearts that he helped develop. In the future, scientists may be able to 3D print real organs using similar technology.

A WARM EMBRACE THAT SAVES LIVES

Premature babies need special equipment to keep them warm. In some places, access to this equipment is limited, and millions of babies die each year. Jane Chen shows an invention that could keep these infants warm—a design that's safe, portable, and low-cost.

PRINTING A HUMAN KIDNEY

There are too few organ donors and thousands of people waiting for transplants. Surgeon Anthony Atala demonstrates an experiment that could someday solve the organ-donor problem: a 3D printer that uses living cells to produce a transplantable kidney.

A TEST FOR PARKINSON'S WITH A PHONE CALL

Parkinson's disease affects 6.3 million people worldwide but there's no way to detect it early. Max Little demonstrates a simple, cheap tool that is able to detect Parkinson's with 99 percent accuracy—in a 30-second phone call.

A What is the theme of the playlist? Circle the best answer.

a new healthcare technology **b** saving babies' lives **c** helping sufferers of disease

B Which speakers most likely said the following? Circle the correct answer.

1 "But what if patients could do this test at home? Now, that would actually save on a difficult trip to the clinic … No expensive staff time required."

a Jane Chen **b** Anthony Atala **c** Max Little

2 "He looks like he's resting peacefully, but in fact he's struggling to stay alive because he can't regulate his own body temperature."

a Jane Chen **b** Anthony Atala **c** Max Little

3 "The problem is, not enough people agree to be donors upon their deaths."

a Jane Chen **b** Anthony Atala **c** Max Little

C Decide which talk you most want to watch. Watch it online at www.ted.com.

3E

WRITING A letter to a health tech company

A Read the sample letter about a technological solution for people who spend long hours at their desks.

Dear Lifestyle Health Products,

Write two paragraphs. In the first paragraph, describe the health problem.

People who sit at their desks for long periods of time are in danger of having more heart attacks and strokes than people who are active. They are often very focused on their work. As a result, they forget about the need to stand up and walk around from time to time.

Use words to express cause and result.

In the second paragraph, describe the benefits of this product.

One way to help them is to provide a wearable device for their wrist that monitors how long they have been sitting. Every half an hour, for example, it could beep to remind them to take a walk or do some exercises. This could be a very good way to help prevent heart attacks and strokes as well as obesity.

Use some new words from this unit.

Conclude with an overall reason why your product will be helpful.

Sincerely,
Jane Robinson

B Think about a group of people you know that might need some help with maintaining a healthy lifestyle. Write a short letter to a health tech company. Explain the problem and suggest a way to help them.

1 Describe the health problem.

2 What difficulties do these people have in their daily lives?

3 How could technology help to make their lives easier?

4 What are the possible applications for the solution you're offering?

C Now write your paragraph. Then complete the checklist below.

- ☐ Did you use the correct greeting and closing?
- ☐ Did you use correct spelling and punctuation?
- ☐ Did you use some new words from this unit?
- ☐ Did you describe how technology could help?

4 Designing the Web

4A

VOCABULARY Describing website features

A Match the definitions to the words on the right.

1 copy data from the Internet onto a computer	○	○	**a** browse
2 a design or symbol that represents a company	○	○	**b** button
3 an opinion of a product or website	○	○	**c** function
4 type in your password to enter a website	○	○	**d** log in
5 skim websites to find which ones are relevant	○	○	**e** logo
6 an icon that you can click to select a command	○	○	**f** review
7 a feature on a website such as "search" or "find"	○	○	**g** download

B Complete the information. Circle the correct words.

WE HAVE A NEW WEBSITE!

[1](**Log in** / **Review**) with your username and password and click the *Enter* [2](**logo** / **button**) to access our site. You can use the search [3](**function** / **logo**) to look for something you want, or [4](**browse** / **button**) our most popular news stories. Like something you see? Click on the [5](**download** / **review**) button and save it to your computer. Don't forget to head to our [6](**logo** / **review**) section. We want to know what you think about our new look. Your feedback is valuable to us!

LISTENING Designing websites

A ▶ **4.1** Listen. What aspects of website design does the speaker focus on?

☐ background ☐ headings ☐ images
☐ feedback ☐ icons ☐ logo

B ▶ **4.1** Listen again. How does the speaker suggest improving each one? Complete the sentences.

1 Use different fonts and ________________ for headings.

2 Change images once a ________________.

3 Use icons for the key ________________ on your website.

COMMUNICATION Talking about decisions

A Complete the conversation. Number the sentences (**1–7**) in the correct order.

a __1__ Is that a new camera?

b ______ Did you also check out the company's website?

c ______ Well, I compared reviews on several models on different websites.

d ______ How did you decide which one to get?

e ______ Yeah, I bought it online a few days ago.

f ______ Yes, I did. I watched some of their promotional videos.

g ______ Wow! All your research was worth it; it looks great.

B Answer the questions using your own words.

1 What gadget have you bought recently?

____

2 How did you decide which one to buy?

____

3 What advice would you give to people who want to buy this gadget?

____

4B

LANGUAGE FOCUS Making comparisons

A Complete the sentences. Use the words provided.

1 My new computer is much faster than my old one.

My old computer isn't as ______________ my new one. (fast)

2 This laptop is heavier than my tablet.

My tablet ______________ my laptop. (light)

3 These speakers aren't as good as those headphones.

These headphones ______________ those speakers. (good)

4 This camera is cheaper than all the other cameras.

This camera is ______________ one on the market. (cheap)

5 The features on this phone are different from the ones on my old phone.

The features on this phone aren't ______________ the ones on my old phone. (same)

B Complete the sentences using your own words.

1 ______________ are easier to carry than ______________.

2 ______________ isn't as expensive as ______________.

3 ______________ is almost the same as ______________, except for the price.

4 ______________ are much more expensive than ______________.

C Read the descriptions. Match the sentences with the correct items. Write **A**, **B**, or **C**.

Item	A 		B 		C 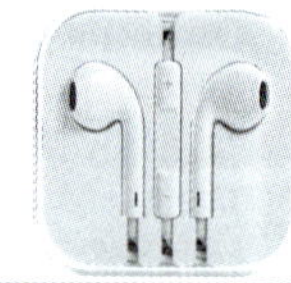	
Description	• $599 • Good for musicians • Quite heavy		• $179 • Good for home listening • Comfortable		• $59 • Good for sports • Lightweight	
Rating	**Overall**	**8.1**	**Overall**	**7.9**	**Overall**	**7.3**
	• Design	8.0	• Design	8.0	• Design	9.0
	• Features	7.0	• Features	7.5	• Features	7.0
	• Sound	9.5	• Sound	9.0	• Sound	6.0
	• Value	8.0	• Value	7.0	• Value	7.0

1 ________ They aren't the cheapest, but they have the best overall rating.

2 ________ They have the best features, and they are very comfortable to use.

3 ________ They have the best design, and they are good for jogging.

4 ________ They have the best sound quality, but they are pretty heavy.

5 ________ They are the cheapest, but they don't have very good sound quality.

LISTENING FOCUS Linking

A ▶ **4.2** Notice how a word ending with an /r/ sound links with the following vowel sound.

This computer is **faster and** easier to use than other models.

More and more are people going online to compare products.

B ▶ **4.3** Read the sentences below. Draw lines to show where the words are linked with an /r/ sound. Listen and check your answers.

1 The best feature is the sound quality.

2 There were other headphones in the review.

3 I'm looking for a cheap but stylish pair.

4 These headphones are good for outdoor use.

5 Each product received an overall score out of ten.

6 This one is more expensive than the others.

C ▶ **4.4** Listen to the conversation. Draw lines to show where the words are linked with an /r/ sound.

A: How's your new computer? Is it better than your old one?

B: It's faster and easier to use! I bought it online.

A: Really? Is it cheaper online?

B: Yes, it's more expensive to buy one in a store.

A: Wow! I never knew that. I should look online more often!

4C

READING

Read the passage and answer the questions.

Here are four easy dos and don'ts that will help you create a website that is fun and easy to use.

A Avoid cluttered pages. Use white space

Most people reading your page will just be scanning it to see if what they're looking for is on it. So it's important to target the information they need first and present it clearly. Don't fill your page with too much unwanted information.

B Include a search box

Many people have a very specific idea of what they are looking for. It might be a specific product or a name, for example, and they don't want to waste time scanning through all the pages to find it. A search function is essential as it will allow users to quickly find what they need.

C Don't ask users for too much information

It's useful to know who's visiting your site, but if you ask people too many questions, they'll just give up. No one wants to spend time completing long forms in order to get to the next page of your site. Even if you have a reason for collecting customer data, try to keep forms short and simple.

D Encourage feedback and questions

You can use your website to build a community of people who share the same interests. Encourage their participation by offering them a way to post comments and send you their questions. This is especially important for websites that sell products or services.

In conclusion, always keep your users' experience in mind and aim for clear and easy-to-use design features to make your website a winner!

The best-designed websites often have a lot of white space.

A Choose the best title for the passage.

a Making Money Online **b** Four Great Websites **c** How to Make a Great Website

B Read the comments from a website's visitors. Which rule does each of the following break? Write the correct letter (**A–D**).

1 "There's no place for visitors to write their opinions." ________

2 "The information given is too long and wordy." ________

3 "There is too much text and too many pictures." ________

4 "There's no way to ask for more information about the products." ________

5 "Why do they need my email address?" ________

6 "I had to scroll through every page to find what I was looking for." ________

LISTENING

A ▶ **4.5** Listen. What are the two people talking about?

a Greg found a website where he bought some cheap headphones.

b Greg visited a website but didn't like the headphones.

c Greg went online to buy some headphones but didn't like the website.

B ▶ **4.5** Listen again. Did Greg have a positive or negative experience of the website features listed below? Circle **P** for positive or **N** for negative.

1	photos	**P**	**N**
2	descriptions	**P**	**N**
3	search box	**P**	**N**
4	navigation	**P**	**N**
5	order form	**P**	**N**
6	contact information	**P**	**N**
7	feedback form	**P**	**N**

C Which rules in the passage would be useful advice for the website Greg visited? Check [✓] all that apply.

a avoid cluttered pages, use white space ☐

b don't ask users for too much information ☐

c include a search box ☐

d encourage feedback and questions ☐

VOCABULARY BUILDING

A Complete the sentences using the words in the box.

attached to	encourage	impact	frustrating	spam

1 What new technology has had a high ______________ on your life?

2 Which tech device are you most ______________?

3 Isn't it ______________ to get so much junk mail every day?

4 Do you have a(n) ______________ blocker on your email?

5 Does your employer actively ______________ you to give feedback on your job?

B Read the definitions below. Then complete the sentences using the correct form of the words in **bold**.

attach: (*v.*) to add or join one thing to another thing

attached to: (*adj.*) fond of something or someone

attachment: (*n.*) something that is attached to something else

1 The girl was very ______________ her kitten and was very sad when it got lost.

2 Please reply to this email and ______________ a copy of your resume.

3 I'm sending three ______________ with this email.

C Answer the questions using your own words.

1 What was your most frustrating experience while shopping online?

____

2 What do you do to avoid getting spam in your emails?

____

3 What's the most encouraging advice you've received on social media?

____

TEDTALKS

4D

TED PLAYLIST

A group of schoolchildren use computers during a lesson.

IDEO's David Kelley says that product design has become much less about the hardware and more about the user experience. He's developing computer interfaces that adapt to human behavior and shows a video of this new, broader approach.

Linda Liukas is encouraging kids to see computers not as mechanical, boring, and complicated but as colorful, expressive machines they can play with. In this talk, she invites us to imagine a world where children will grow up to be optimistic about technology.

In this funny and enlightening talk, *New York Times* journalist David Pogue takes a close look at the unnecessarily complicated design of computer software. He highlights some of the worst mistakes developers make, and provides encouraging examples of products that get it right.

A Match the title of each TED Talk to the correct speaker.

1 Simplicity Sells	○ ○	**a** David Kelley
2 A Delightful Way to Teach Kids about Computers	○ ○	**b** Linda Liukas
3 Human-centered Design	○ ○	**c** David Pogue

B What is the theme of the playlist? Circle the best answer.

a how we interact with computers

b how to design computer software for children

c how computer software is improving

C Which speakers most likely said the following? Circle the correct answer.

1 "Unless we give them tools to build with computers, we are raising only consumers instead of creators."

a David Kelley **b** Linda Liukas **c** David Pogue

2 "Remember, the hard part is not deciding what features to add, it's deciding what to leave out."

a David Kelley **b** Linda Liukas **c** David Pogue

D Decide which talk you most want to watch. Watch it online at www.ted.com.

4E

WRITING Writing a review

A Read the sample review of an app.

Write one paragraph. Start by describing the website or product.

I downloaded an app to search for new movies. I really love sci-fi movies, so I want to be able to search for new sci-fi that are available online as soon as they come out. This app updates me with the latest movies and also tells me which ones are popular right now. It's more up-to-date than most of the other similar products on the market. The app downloads quickly and is easy to use. The main problem I had with this app was that there was no search box. It took me a long time to find the movies I liked.

Use some new words from this unit.

Then say why you liked this product and what its advantages are.

Describe one design flaw.

B Choose a website or an app that you have used. Answer the questions to plan your review.

1 What is the product for?

2 What did you like about it? What did you expect?

3 What are the advantages of it?

4 What were the design flaws?

C Now write your paragraph. Then complete the checklist below.

☐ Did you use correct spelling and punctuation?

☐ Did you use some new words from this unit?

☐ Did you compare different things?

☐ Did you explain how to improve the design?

5 Community Builders

5A

VOCABULARY Making communities better

Complete the sentences using the words in the box. One word is extra.

community **empowers** **enhancing** **entrepreneurs** **facilities** **underprivileged**

1 She started a nonprofit organization for ________ children to express themselves through art.

2 His success story inspired everyone in the ________.

3 Education ________ you. It gives you the tools you need to succeed in life.

4 The government spent a lot of money upgrading the ________ in the library complex.

5 Steve Jobs, Mark Zuckerberg, and Bill Gates are all ________ who started small but made it big.

LISTENING Creating green spaces

A ▷ 5.1 Listen. The two speakers are probably ___.

a politicians **b** neighbors **c** gardeners

B ▷ 5.1 Listen to the conversation again. Answer the questions.

1 What is focus of the project?

a building communities **b** developing urban gardens **c** eating more healthily

2 Where will this project be carried out?

a on building rooftops **b** people's backyards **c** at the library

3 Who can participate in this project?

a library members **b** local residents **c** friends

4 What are the advantages of this project? Check [✓] all that apply.

a You can grow your own vegetables. ☐

b There will be fewer empty buildings. ☐

c There will be more greenery in the city. ☐

d It will help reduce pollution. ☐

e It's a great way to make friends. ☐

f People can help and learn from one another. ☐

COMMUNICATION Talking about my community

A Complete the conversation. Number the sentences (**1–7**) in the correct order.

a ______ Really? Maybe you could suggest that your local council build one.

b ______ Well, it's quite peaceful and friendly.

c ______ I guess I could. Maybe if everyone at school supported the idea, they might consider it.

d __1__ Hi, I heard you recently moved to a new neighborhood. What's it like?

e ______ That's fantastic. I have to take a bus to the next town if I want to go to the library.

f ______ That's nice! Are there many facilities?

g ______ Yes, there's a supermarket and a library.

B Answer the questions using your own words.

1 What is your community like?

____

2 What kind of facilities do you have?

____

3 What would you improve in your community?

____

5B

LANGUAGE FOCUS Using the passive voice

A Rewrite each sentence using the passive form.

1 You can recycle rainwater from the roof.

Rainwater from the roof can be recycled.

2 They turned unused land into urban gardens.

Unused land ______________________________

3 Someone designed the cars to run on solar power.

The cars ______________________________

4 They converted a landfill into a skateboard park.

A landfill ______________________________

5 They built tunnels to divert traffic underground.

Tunnels ______________________________

B Complete the information with the passive form of the words provided.

The High Line, built in 1934, was an overhead railroad track in Manhattan, New York, which [1] ________________ (use) to transport cargo into the city. However, when rail traffic started to decline, it was decided that the train tracks [2] ________________ (need) any more and the city decided it should [3] ________________ (tear down) and demolished. An organization called the Friends of the High Line [4] ________________ (form) to fight against the demolition. A competition [5] ________________ (hold) to find the best idea for the site. Ten years later, the High Line [6] ________________ (redesign) as a beautiful urban park and garden. The old train tracks [7] ________________ (convert) into a place where people can [8] ________________ (surround) by green trees and flowers. Today, the High Line [9] ________________ (visit) by hundreds of New Yorkers looking for some green space in the urban jungle. Further work on the project [10] ________________ (plan), with ideas for museums, art spaces, and other facilities.

C Answer the questions.

1 What has changed recently in your city or neighborhood? ________________

____

2 What kind of environmental improvements have been introduced? ________________

____

3 What kinds of changes have been most beneficial to the city? ________________

____

LISTENING FOCUS Word stress: *can* and *can't*

A 5.2 Listen to the sentences. Notice the difference in pronunciation between *can* and *can't*. *Can* is usually unstressed, and the vowel sound is reduced. *Can't* is usually stressed.

A bridge **can** be constructed.

The river **can** be cleaned.

The walls **can't** be painted.

The streets **can't** be repaired.

B 5.3 Listen. Circle the correct word to complete the sentences.

1 The water (**can** / **can't**) be used.

2 Trees (**can** / **can't**) be planted.

3 It (**can** / **can't**) be improved.

4 A sports center (**can** / **can't**) be built.

5 They (**can** / **can't**) be replaced.

C 5.4 Listen and write the sentences you hear.

1 ________________

2 ________________

3 ________________

4 ________________

5 ________________

5C

READING

Read the passage and answer the questions.

One of Tusingwire's projects was a playground made from recycled materials.

1 Ruganzu Bruno Tusingwire is an eco-artist from Uganda. Orphaned as young child, he grew up in the countryside, surrounded by mountains and nature. Later, he moved to the capital city of Kampala and was shocked by the amount of waste all around him. There was so much waste it was becoming unmanageable. He realized it was important for everyone to work together as a community to reduce and recycle waste.

2 He started working on eco-art projects with some of his fellow students. They collected plastic bottles to make sculptures. They went to festivals and other public places and invited the public to help them finish the work by collecting more bottles. At first, people didn't understand what they were doing. But later, they joined in enthusiastically in creating art from waste.

3 Even though his projects were successful and popular, Tusingwire wanted to do more. He didn't only want to create art, he wanted to ensure that his project would create significant long-term benefits for his community. He wanted to help underprivileged children growing up in the slums, so he decided to create a playground for children. He talked with members of the community, including teachers, parents, and children. They all helped to collect bottles and other useable trash to make the playground, which they designed and built together.

4 The eco-art amusement park is a place where children can explore, climb, and play among the brightly colored climbing frames, life-sized board games, and swings—all made out of recycled tires, plastic bottles, and other trash. The children's smiles and shouts of laughter are proof of the success of the project.

5 Tusingwire's goal is to create many more similar amusement parks in other parts of Uganda. "Art is unifying," Tusingwire explains. "We can use what is around us to create treasure, employment opportunities, and make the environment better. There is a wonderful world of possibilities before us."

A What is the passage mainly about?

a A project to help raise money for underprivileged children in Uganda.

b The growing trash problem in Uganda's countryside.

c A young man who started a project to recycle waste and help a community.

B Circle the correct answer.

1 What inspired Tusingwire to start his eco-art projects?

- **a** He saw how much trash there was in the countryside where he grew up.
- **b** He helped clean up after a local festival and didn't know what to do with the trash.
- **c** He was shocked by the amount of trash he saw when he moved to the city.

2 How was Tusingwire's eco-art playground different from his earlier projects?

- **a** The playground was successful and popular.
- **b** The playground was more than just a piece of art.
- **c** The playgroud was built entirely from recycled waste.

3 What is Tusingwire's future goal?

- **a** to teach others around the world about recycling
- **b** to help people in his community get jobs
- **c** to create similar parks around the country

LISTENING

A ▶ 5.5 Listen. What is the main purpose of the art exhibition?

a to persuade people to reduce trash

b to show different ways to recycle trash

c to empower people to create art

B ▶ 5.5 Listen again. Circle **T** for true or **F** for false.

1	The sculptures are made from trash.	**T**	**F**
2	The trash was collected from major cities.	**T**	**F**
3	Angela Pozzi built the sculptures by herself.	**T**	**F**
4	There are 143 billion kilograms of plastic in our oceans.	**T**	**F**
5	Trash in the oceans affects both animals and humans.	**T**	**F**

C Use the information (**a–i**) to complete the Venn diagram.

a It helps underprivileged people.
b It turns trash into art.
c It aims to raise awareness.
d It is an art exhibition held at a zoo.
e Trash was collected from beaches.
f Local communities were involved.
g It was started by an artist.
h It was done in the United States.
i It was done in Uganda.

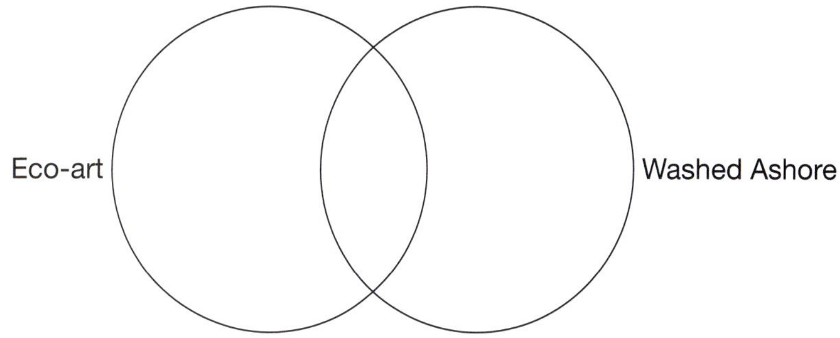

VOCABULARY BUILDING

A Complete the sentences using the words in the box.

dedication	ensure	proof	recruit	significant

1 There is scientific __________ that the amount of trash in the ocean is growing.
2 Community group leaders usually __________ volunteers to help with their projects.
3 Community projects need to __________ that their work will continue after they have left.
4 The volunteers showed great __________ to the recycling campaign.
5 Reducing and recycling trash can have a(n) __________ impact on the environment.

B Some adjectives use the suffix *-ant*. Complete the sentences using the words in the box.

constant	distant	hesitant	vacant

1 The building was abandoned and had been __________ for many years.
2 People were __________ to join at first but now they're very enthusiastic.
3 We heard a __________ crash from several kilometers away.
4 I couldn't sleep because of the __________ noise from the airport.

5D

TED PLAYLIST

Vegetables are grown in the rooftop garden of a city building.

BUILDING A PARK IN THE SKY

New York City was planning to tear down the High Line, an old elevated railroad above the streets of Manhattan, when Robert Hammond and a few friends suggested: Why not make it a park? He talks about how he started a local community organization to save the High Line and make it into a park.

A PARK UNDERNEATH THE HUSTLE AND BUSTLE OF NEW YORK CITY

Dan Barasch and James Ramsey have a crazy plan—to create the Lowline, an underground park the size of a football field underneath New York City. The two are building it in an abandoned trolley bus station, which was last used in 1948. They're using technology to bring sunlight from above-ground to down below.

A GUERILLA GARDENER IN SOUTH CENTRAL LA

Ron Finley plants vegetable gardens in South Central Los Angeles—on abandoned land at the edges of the street. Why? For fun, for beauty, and to offer some alternative to fast food. His long term goal is to make his community a more peaceful and beautiful place to live.

A Match each speaker to the topic of their TED Talk.

1 Robert Hammond ○	○ **a** growing food on city streets
2 Dan Barasch ○	○ **b** creating a park underground
3 Ron Finley ○	○ **c** transforming a railroad

B Which speakers most likely said the following? Circle the correct answer.

1 "I first read about it in the *New York Times*, in an article that said it was going to be demolished."
a Dan Barasch **b** Robert Hammond **c** Ron Finley

2 "A lot of people said to us, 'Oh, it kind of looks like the High Line underground.'"
a Dan Barasch **b** Robert Hammond **c** Ron Finley

3 "I planted a food forest in front of my house."
a Dan Barasch **b** Robert Hammond **c** Ron Finley

C What do all three speakers have in common?

a they created a kind of park **b** they teach new skills to others **c** they used unwanted spaces

D Decide which talk you most want to watch. Watch it online at www.ted.com.

5E

WRITING Making a suggestion

A Read the sample letter to a local city council requesting for a community garden in the neighborhood.

Write two paragraphs. In the first paragraph, describe why you are suggesting this idea.

In the second paragraph, describe the benefits of this project.

Dear Sir/Madam,

I'm writing to suggest the creation of a community garden in my neighborhood. There are many people who live in apartments who don't have gardens but would love to grow their own vegetables. There is also a lot of abandoned land that is not being used. I think that many people would welcome the opportunity to use this land to grow their own food.

The benefits of this would be that the abandoned land is used for a good purpose, community members would get to grow and eat healthy food, and it would improve their sense of community when they work together. In my opinion, it would make our community a happier and healthier place.

Yours sincerely,

Scott

Use some new words from this unit.

Use phrases like "I suggest," "I think," and "In my opinion."

B Write a letter to your city council requesting a new playground for children. Answer the questions to plan your letter.

1 Describe the project.

2 Why is it needed?

3 What are the benefits?

4 How will your neighborhood change?

C Now write your letter. Then complete the checklist below.

- ☐ Did you use correct spelling and punctuation?
- ☐ Did you use some new words from this unit?
- ☐ Did you use passive forms?
- ☐ Did you explain how your project will improve the community?

6 Clear Communication

6A

VOCABULARY Using communication collocations

A Complete the paragraph using the words in the box.

have	having	make	making	post	write	writing

Whether you're [1]________________ a conversation, [2] ________________ a speech, or [3] ________________ an email, it is important to adapt your communication style to the medium you are using. When you [4] ________________ a meeting, your communication style will usually be more formal than when you [5] ________________ a phone call. Similarly, when you [6] ________________ an update on social media, it will usually be simpler and more direct than when you [7] ________________ a letter.

B Correct the mistake in each sentence.

1 Have you had to give a phone call in English?

2 How often do you make letters to your friends?

3 Do you prefer giving text messages or emails?

4 When was the last time you posted a speech in public?

5 Do you sometimes make photos online?

LISTENING Communication styles

A ▶ **6.1** Listen to an expert giving advice to managers about communication. What are the three tips the expert gives? Complete the sentences.

1 Use different ________________ channels.

2 Use a ________________ that creates a supportive atmosphere.

3 Show that you appreciate your team's ________________ .

B ▶ **6.1** Listen again. Would the speaker agree with the following statements? Circle **Y** for yes or **N** for no.

1 It's okay for managers to hold group meetings. **Y** **N**

2 One-to-one meetings are a waste of time. **Y** **N**

3 Managers should use a commanding tone. **Y** **N**

4 A manager should thank staff for their time after meetings. **Y** **N**

COMMUNICATION Talking about communication preferences

A Complete the conversations using the phrases in the box.

I saw it on YouTube.	**I posted them on Facebook.**
I'll send it in an email.	**You can buy them online.**

1 **A:** Have you checked out our school's new website?

B: No, can you send me the link?

A: Sure. ____________________

2 **A:** Did you see my photos?

B: Which photos? Did you send them by email?

A: No, ____________________

3 **A:** Did you get tickets for the concert?

B: Not yet. Where do I get them?

A: ____________________

4 **A:** Look at this video. It shows you how to play the guitar!

B: Cool! Where did you find it?

A: ____________________

B Complete the conversation. Circle the correct words.

A: Hey, Martin, [1] (**check** / **share**) this out!

B: Hi, Lisa. What's up?

A: My friend [2] (**checked** / **posted**) a video of his band on YouTube. Want to see?

B: Sure. Wow, they sound great! Can you send me the [3] (**post** / **link**)?

A: Of course. If you really like it, could you [4] (**share** / **post**) a comment? They'll really appreciate it.

B: No problem, I'll [5] (**share** / **check**) the link with my friends too.

6B

LANGUAGE FOCUS Describing types of communicators

A Complete the conversation. Circle the correct words.

A: Have you told the boss you want [1] (**to quit** / **quitting**) yet?

B: Not yet. I'm planning [2] (**to send** / **sending**) him an email today.

A: An email? I'd strongly recommend [3] (**to talk** / **talking**) to him face to face.

B: But I'm worried that he'll try to persuade me [4] (**to stay** / **staying**). An email seems much easier.

A: Well, it's your decision, but I know he'll dislike [5] (**to hear** / **hearing**) this kind of news via email.

B Rewrite each sentence so that it has the same meaning. Use the words provided.

1 I don't usually write long emails. (avoid)

____

2 I think you should create your own blog. (recommend)

____

3 Video chatting is a good way to stay in touch with friends who live far away. (help)

____

4 A smartphone means you can stay in touch wherever you are. (allow)

____

C Complete the sentences using your own words.

1 I usually ______________________ my friends every day.

2 I like ______________ my family because ______________.

3 ______________ allows me to ______________ with my co-workers.

4 I avoid ______________ because ______________.

5 ______________ helps me ______________.

LISTENING FOCUS Intonation when agreeing and disagreeing

A 6.2 We usually use rising intonation when we disagree with someone. We often use falling intonation when we agree. Listen and repeat what you hear.

A: I really don't like group meetings. **B:** Really? I find them really useful.

A: I really don't like group meetings. **B:** Yeah. They can be really boring.

B 6.3 Listen to the sentences. Draw arrows to show rising or falling intonation in B's replies. Listen and check your answers.

1 **A:** Email is so old-fashioned. **B:** Yeah. I never use it these days.

2 **A:** I really don't like using Facebook. **B:** Really? I use it every day.

3 **A:** I hate speaking in public. **B:** Yeah? I actually quite enjoy it.

C 6.4 Listen to the intonation in the sentences below. Do you think the person is agreeing or disagreeing with someone? Circle **A** for agreeing or **D** for disagreeing.

1 I thought it was really interesting. **A** **D**

2 I thought it was too short. **A** **D**

3 I found the end part the most interesting. **A** **D**

4 Her delivery was really good. **A** **D**

D 6.5 Listen to the full conversation and check your answers in **C**.

6C

READING

Read the passage and answer the questions below.

1 Maddalena Bearzi is a marine biologist. She believes there are many things that scientists can do to help the general public understand difficult scientific concepts. She has four simple suggestions to help scientists make science more accessible to the rest of us.

2 Firstly, scientists need to find ways of explaining complex things in everyday terms. They should learn from some of the great scientific communicators, such as Albert Einstein or Carl Sagan, and relate information to everyday situations so their audience can better grasp any complex concepts.

3 A scientist should also assume that their readers or viewers are as smart and curious as they are. The average person just doesn't know what a scientist knows. There is no doubt that scientists and the public often have different communication styles. So scientists need to know how to talk to their audience without boring them with scientific talk!

Maddalena Bearzi believes scientists need to communicate better with the general public.

4 Science writers can learn a lot from fiction writers. They should share their adventures in the lab using engaging and inspiring plots, odd characters, or mysteries. True stories can easily be written to sound more like "fiction" to gain popular appeal. If scientists can talk about their personal feelings and experiences, it will make their stories come alive.

5 Finally, scientists should avoid using graphs and tables if they can, and, where possible, not use text on their presentation slides. Audiences should be engaged with exciting images or even cartoon strips to lighten up a talk.

6 The goal of a scientist, as either writer or speaker, is to be accessible to everyone regardless of their background. Now, more than ever, it is important to recognize these gaps by writing or speaking in a way that bridges them.

A Match the headings to the correct paragraphs.

1 Paragraph 2 ○	○	**a** Use pictures if you can.
2 Paragraph 3 ○	○	**b** Use simple and easy-to-understand language.
3 Paragraph 4 ○	○	**c** Tell interesting stories.
4 Paragraph 5 ○	○	**d** Don't underestimate your audience.

B Would Maddelena Bearzi agree with the following statements? Circle **Y** for yes or **N** for no.

1 Albert Einstein was good at communicating with the public.	**Y**	**N**
2 Scientists should realize most people are not as smart as they are.	**Y**	**N**
3 Most scientists communicate in a different style to the general public.	**Y**	**N**
4 Scientific ideas can be communicated effectively through stories.	**Y**	**N**
5 Scientists should use graphs whenever they can.	**Y**	**N**

LISTENING

A ▶ **6.6** Listen. Which sentence best describes the book?

a It is a detailed description of plants and animals.

b It combines personal stories with scientific descriptions.

c It is a handbook for how to teach science.

B ▶ **6.6** Listen again. Circle **T** for true, **F** for false, or **NG** for not given.

1 The speaker found the book interesting.	**T**	**F**	**NG**
2 The author engages her readers by asking them questions.	**T**	**F**	**NG**
3 In the book, the author talks about her childhood.	**T**	**F**	**NG**
4 The book contains photos taken by the author.	**T**	**F**	**NG**
5 The author says her work as a scientist was always exciting.	**T**	**F**	**NG**

C **CRITICAL THINKING** Do you think the author has followed the guidelines given in the reading passage? Give examples to support your answer.

___

___

___

VOCABULARY BUILDING

A Complete the sentences using the words in the box.

analogy	concise	last	span	technical

1 The article included a very long and detailed explanation. It wasn't a very ______________ description.

2 His argument was too difficult to understand. He used a lot of scientific and ______________ words.

3 The first study only lasted two years, but the second one had a time ______________ of ten years.

4 My teacher compared sound waves to waves in the ocean, which was a useful ______________.

5 When carrying out community projects, it's important that the changes will ______________.

B Complete the sentences using the words in **bold**.

attention span: the amount of time you can concentrate
life span: the length of your life
time span: a length or period of time

1 The average two-year-old has a(n) ______________ of about five minutes.

2 Elephants have a(n) ______________ of up to 70 years.

3 Future research may focus on specific areas over a shorter ______________.

C Answer the questions using your own words.

1 What kind of analogy could a scientist use to explain the size of the solar system?

____

2 Do you have a short or long attention span? Why do you say so?

____

3 What is the average life span of the people in your country?

____

A speaker shows a slide at the Warsaw Medical Congress for Young Scientists.

TEDTALKS

6D

TED PLAYLIST

The Large Hadron Collider (LHC) at CERN

CERN'S SUPERCOLLIDER

Physicist Brian Cox has two jobs: working with the Large Hadron Collider at CERN, and explaining science to the general public. In this talk, Cox brings us along on a tour of this massive project, and explains the LHC's search for new particles in an engaging, accessible way.

THE MOST MYSTERIOUS STAR IN THE UNIVERSE

Something massive, with roughly 1,000 times the area of Earth, is blocking the light coming from a distant star known as KIC 8462852, and nobody is quite sure what it is. In this talk, Tabetha Boyajian gives us a look at how scientists search for and test hypotheses when faced with the unknown.

HOW WE'LL FIND LIFE ON OTHER PLANETS

Astronomer Aomawa Shields searches for clues that life might exist elsewhere in the universe by examining the atmospheres of distant exoplanets. When she isn't exploring the heavens, the classically trained actor looks for ways to engage young women in the sciences using theater, writing, and visual art.

A What is the theme of this playlist?

a discoveries in science **b** exploring the solar system **c** combining science and art

B Check [✓] the correct column(s).

Which speaker(s)...	Brian Cox	Tabetha Boyajian	Aomawa Shields
1 is interested in a mysterious star?			
2 tries to help women scientists?			
3 talks about a very big science project?			
4 asks questions about life on other planets?			
5 educates the public during their free time?			

C Decide which talk you most want to watch. Watch it online at www.ted.com.

6E

WRITING Giving an explanation

A Read the sample answer about a description of a game.

Remember to explain any steps carefully and to emphasize key points.

My favorite board game is Scrabble. Imagine creating a giant crossword: players build this "crossword" by adding one word to it at a time.

Scrabble can be played by two to four people. You need a set of small wooden or plastic squares—each one has a letter printed on it. Different letters have different values; for example, A is worth one point, and Q is worth 10 points. Each player gets seven letter squares. You use a board that is marked with squares. The board has colored squares that can double or triple the points of a letter, or word, placed on that square.

The aim of the game is to form words by placing your letters on the board to gain points for each one. The winner is the person with the most points at the end of the game.

Make your main message short and clear.

B Describe a game or sport that you like. Answer the questions to plan your description.

1 What is the name of the game?

2 What are the rules of the game?

3 Is there an analogy you can use to explain the game?

4 How do you win the game?

C Now write your description. Then complete the checklist below.

☐ Did you use correct spelling and punctuation?

☐ Did you use some new words from this unit?

☐ Did you explain the rules of the game or sport?

☐ Did you use analogies to describe your game or sport?

Audio Scripts

1.1 In today's podcast, we're going to look at three easy ways for companies to encourage employees to become volunteers.

The best way to encourage volunteering at work is to offer paid time for volunteering. This could mean that employees can take one day per month—or more—and donate their time as a volunteer without losing any of their salary. This shows that a company really cares about volunteering and considers it an important use of employees' time.

Another thing companies can do is to compile a list of volunteer organizations and charities that need help. You can make sure that these organizations fit with your company profile and at the same time offer employees more information and choices to choose from.

Finally, an important part of any volunteer program is to recognize and value the work that volunteers have done. Publish an article about them in the company newsletter, or organize a special lunch to acknowledge those who have volunteered.

Any or all of these strategies will have an enormous impact on the way volunteering is seen in the company and will inspire people to continue working there. Volunteering is a way to help people develop new skills and learn to get along with each other. This allows them to work better as a team, and makes a positive impact on the local community.

1.2 What do you do as a volunteer?; Whaddaya do as a volunteer?; What did you do as a volunteer?; Whadidja do as a volunteer?

1.3 **1.** What kind of work did you do?; **2.** How did you get to work?; **3.** Who do you ask for help?; **4.** What do you like about being a volunteer?

1.4 **1.** Where do you work?; **2.** Do you enjoy working there?; **3.** What did you help them with?; **4.** Do you have people to help you?

1.5 Charities that work to end poverty and hunger in developing countries have to make sure that the money reaches the people who need it most. However, they also have to make sure that the money has a long-term impact on these people.

That's what a charity called Heifer International does. Heifer International was founded over 70 years ago by Dan West—a farmer from the United States. Instead of giving money and food to communities, Heifer International donates animals—cows, sheep, water buffalo, chickens, and even bees—to families so that communities can learn to manage their own food source. The organization trains people on how to take care of these animals and how to use them to make wool, cheese, or honey.

An important part of the project is that whenever an animal gives birth, the family that owns it has to give the first female baby animal to another poor family and help them learn how to take care of it. This way, the knowledge and skills are passed on throughout the community and keep growing.

The ultimate goal of Heifer international is to end world hunger by creating communities around the world that have their own sustainable food sources.

2.1 Since the rise of the Internet in the 1990s, blogs have become a popular way for people to express their views on different topics to a much wider audience than ever before.

Blogging started to become popular after the first blogging websites were launched in 1999. The same year also saw the first use of the word "blog"—a short form of the word "weblog." Shortly after, the verb "to blog" and the noun "blogger" also became commonly used in English.

Since the turn of the century, many different types of blogs have arisen. Many people keep personal blogs that serve as a kind of online diary. Other blogs focus on a particular subject such as cars, technology, or fashion. According to Google, music is the most common topic for blogs like these. Many companies also have blogs, either for internal communication, or often as a way of marketing their products or services to customers.

Estimates suggest that there are now around 150 million blogs on the Internet, and the number is increasing. It's thought that two new blogs are created somewhere in the world every second!

▶ **2.2** Do you think life in the future will be **better**, or **worse**?; Do you think robots will make life **easier**, or more **difficult**?

▶ **2.3** **1.** Do you think people will have **more** free time, or **less**?; **2.** Will cities become **larger**, or **smaller**? **3.** Do you think air travel will be **faster**, or **just the same**? **4.** Will the world population **increase**, or **decrease**?

▶ **2.4** Today's podcast is all about fashion! How do fashion trends get started and who ultimately influences what we buy and wear?

A lot of fashion trends start on the street. That's right, they're styles that are worn by ordinary people who have an innovative idea—whether it's a new kind of hairstyle—or a new way to layer t-shirts. Other people notice them and start to copy their style. Street style often ends up being copied by the big fashion designers!

Another big influence is fashion bloggers. Talented fashion bloggers have their own unique styles. They take photos of themselves wearing different clothes and accessories and post the photos online. They can often develop a huge audience. Italian fashion blogger Chiara Ferragni, for example, has more than 3 million Instagram followers.

With the rise of social media, people's fashion is also becoming increasingly influenced by their friends and social peer groups. It's become so much easier to share a picture of your latest fashion idea with friends instantly. A new style idea can go viral in just a few minutes and be shared with thousands of people in just a few hours.

There's no doubt that fashion today is far more varied than ever before. People look for inspiration from a wide range of sources. As social media tools enable us to express ourselves and develop our own unique style, more and more people are becoming trendsetters, not just trend followers.

▶ **3.1** Medical technology is improving all the time. But is it possible that one day our doctors and nurses will be entirely replaced by machines? Doctors already make heavy use of computers. Computers can scan and analyze huge quantities of patients' data in a very short time and come up with a diagnosis. Some believe that this technology could be developed further. A medical robot could perform a series of routine tests on a patient, such as checking blood pressure, and then recommend a treatment. This could be especially useful for patients who visit the doctor regularly with a chronic condition such as heart disease. The human doctor would then have more time to specialize in illnesses that are more difficult to treat.

Many believe, however, that robots could never completely replace human doctors. Only humans have the ability to include emotional and psychological factors in their assessment of a patient's condition. What's more, dealing with patients' anxieties and worries about a condition is thought to be a key part of a doctor's role. It's unlikely that robots could ever provide the counseling and emotional support that human doctors can.

▶ **3.2** **1. A:** When do you usually play tennis? **B:** I usually play tennis on **Sundays**.; **2. A:** What do you usually do on Sundays? **B:** I usually **play tennis** on Sundays.

▶ **3.3** **1. A:** When are you having lunch with Daniel? **B:** I'm having lunch with him **tomorrow**.; **2. A:** Who are you having lunch with tomorrow? **B:** I'm having lunch with **Daniel** tomorrow.; **3. A:** Are you having dinner with Daniel tomorrow? **B:** No. I'm having **lunch** with him tomorrow.

▶ **3.4** **1.** What do you usually eat for breakfast?; **2.** When do you go to the gym?; **3.** Who bought you that watch?; **4.** What did the doctor tell you?

▶ **3.5** As wearable tech devices become more and more popular, there's an increasing number of devices that aim to help people with health conditions.

One of these is a wearable sensor patch that you can attach to your arm like a small adhesive bandage. The sensor collects data about your overall health, such as how many hours you sleep, what your heart rate is, and how fast you are breathing. It can also collect data from the sweat on the surface of your skin and can tell you about your blood sugar level, or whether you are drinking enough water. It can send you a summary of this data or send it to your doctor or caregiver.

The sensor is very useful for people with heart diseases, or people who have problems with high cholesterol. It can be used by patients recovering from strokes, or surgeries. It is also useful for monitoring elderly people at home to make sure they are coping well with medication.

However, it is also useful for healthy people who want to monitor their health and prevent conditions such as heart disease or diabetes.

4.1 Keeping your website fresh and up-to-date needn't be a chore! Here are some easy tips on how to improve your website.

The first thing to look at is the way you use headings to focus attention on the main information. You can make information stand out by using headings in different fonts and colors. But don't overload! Too many different styles of fonts and colors will be confusing, and users will soon give up and go to another page.

The second thing to look at is the images. Are they fresh and exciting? People who frequently visit your page don't want to see the same picture every time. Try changing the images once a month so that the page always looks fresh. There are many websites that offer hundreds of photos, many of which are free.

Finally, think about using icons for the key functions on your website. Icons immediately attract the eye and make the page look exciting and fun. You can use icons for functions such as "download" or "add to your shopping basket." There are several websites where you can download free icons. Using icons will make your website look professional and easy to navigate.

These small design tweaks can help to refresh your website and keep users interested in visiting your website again!

4.2 This computer is faster and easier to use than other models. More and more are people going online to compare products.

4.3 **1.** The best feature is the sound quality.; **2.** There were other headphones in the review.; **3.** I'm looking for a cheap but stylish pair.; **4.** These headphones are good for outdoor use.; **5.** Each product received an overall score out of ten. **6.** This one is more expensive than the others.

4.4

M: How's your new computer? Is it better than your old one?

W: It's faster and easier to use! I bought it online.

M: Really? Is it cheaper online?

W: Yes, it's more expensive to buy one in a store.

M: Wow! I never knew that. I should look online more often!

4.5

W: Hey, Greg! Did you manage to find those new headphones online? Did you buy them?

M: Hi Tina! Well yes and no. Yes, I found them online, but no I didn't buy them.

W: You didn't! Why not?

M: Well ... there were a couple of different reasons. I managed to find the site and it looked very professional—amazing photos and clear descriptions for all their products. It was easy to use the search box to find the headphones I was looking for, so I found the ones I wanted. But when I clicked on the "buy now" button, I had to fill out this really long form with all sorts of personal information like my birth date, annual income, and so on.

W: Oh no, that's really frustrating. That's how you end up getting lots of spam.

M: Right! And this made me a bit suspicious, you know, why would they need all this information from me? So I started to look around the site more carefully, and I couldn't find any contact information. What if I sent them my money, and I didn't get my headphones—who would I contact?

W: You're right, that is kind of scary. You should send them a complaint.

M: Hah! That's another thing. There was no way to ask a question or send in a complaint because there was no feedback form or contact information!

W: Hmm...You were right not to buy your headphones from them.

5.1

M: Have you heard about this new urban gardening association?

W: No, what is it?

M: Well, a group of residents are getting together to start urban gardens on the roofs of buildings and train stations. There'll be quite a large number of small plots available and anyone who lives in the area can apply to get one.

W: Oh really? So you can grow your own vegetables and flowers and that type of thing?

M: Exactly! Wouldn't it be great to have home-grown vegetables for your dinner?

W: Wow! That does sound good. I really miss having my own backyard in the city.

M: Yeah, there are so many benefits from this project. It's a really good way to create more greenery in the city.

W: ... and it'll help reduce pollution!

M: You're absolutely right! Plus, it's not just about growing your own food, it's also about building a community so people can learn from each other and help each other.

W: That would be a great way to meet people and make friends. Maybe I could join?

M: Sure! There's a meeting about it at the library this weekend—let's go there together!

▶ **5.2** A bridge can be constructed.; The walls can't be painted.; The river can be cleaned.; The streets can't be repaired.

▶ **5.3** **1.** The water can't be used.; **2.** Trees can be planted.; **3.** It can be improved.; **4.** A sports center can be built.; **5.** They can't be replaced.

▶ **5.4** **1.** This trash can be recycled.; **2.** You can't park here.; **3.** I can't understand what you're saying.; **4.** He can help with the project.; **5.** The park can't be built until summer.

▶ **5.5** Washed Ashore is an art exhibition at the Smithsonian's National Zoo in Washington, D.C. It is designed to raise awareness of how much trash we are throwing into our oceans.

Seen from a distance, these massive sculptures look like brightly colored sea creatures—larger-than-life fish, seals, and jellyfish. But look at them more closely, and you'll be surprised.

The sculptures are entirely made out of trash that has been washed ashore onto our beaches—plastic bottles, plastic bags, containers,and old toothbrushes, amongst many other things.

The project was started by Angela Pozzi, an artist and educator based in Bandon, Oregon. She is dedicated to reducing trash in our oceans. She wants to attract people's attention with the beauty of the sculptures, which then become horrifying as you get close up. It was a real community project. She recruited volunteers to collect trash from the beach and then build the sculptures together.

There are 143 billion kilograms of plastic in the world's oceans, and trash is found everywhere—even on beaches in Alaska. This poses a significant danger to wildlife. When birds or seals eat plastic, they can choke on it and die. When fish eat plastic, it poisons them. This poison is then passed on up the food chain to larger fish and ultimately to us when we eat fish. This art exhibition motivates us all to do more to reduce trash in our oceans.

▶ **6.1** If you're a manager, effective communication is the key to success. Having clear communication will help your team work together effectively, prevent misunderstandings, and ensure your projects run more smoothly. Here are three tips to help you communicate effectively with your team.

First, use different communication channels. Holding a group meeting is fine, and may seem time-efficient, but it is important to remember that some people respond better to individual communication, such as emails and one-to-one meetings. Try to notice which channels work best with which people.

Second, use a tone that creates a relaxed and supportive atmosphere. Although some managers use a more commanding tone, this can sometimes hurt their employees' feelings and cause resentment. Try to use a tone that is friendly but assertive. Avoid sarcasm, and always show a willingness to listen. This will make team members feel involved and more willing to contribute their creative ideas.

And finally, it's important to show that you appreciate your team's efforts and that you are aware of their contributions. If you have a meeting, always thank your staff for their time. If someone contributes a good idea, make sure you praise them for it. This will demonstrate that you are open to ideas and will encourage others to give their opinions, too.

6.2

M: I really don't like group meetings.

W: Really? I find them really useful.

M: I really don't like group meetings.

W: Yeah. They can be really boring.

6.3 **1. M:** Email is so old-fashioned. **W:** Yeah. I never use it these days.; **2. W:** I really don't like using Facebook. **M:** Really? I use it every day.; **3. M:** I hate speaking in public. **W:** Yeah? I actually quite enjoy it.

6.4 **1.** I thought it was really interesting.; **2.** I thought it was too short.; **3.** I found the end part the most interesting.; **4.** Her delivery was really good.

6.5

M: I quite enjoyed that presentation.

W: Yeah. I thought it was really interesting.

M: It was a bit too long though.

W: Did you think so? I thought it was too short.

M: Really? You didn't get bored near the end. I know I did.

W: No. I found the end part the most interesting.

M: Okay. She was a great speaker though.

W: Yeah. Her delivery was really good.

6.6 "Lab Girl" is a book about plant science, written by Hope Jahren—a professor of geobiology at the University of Hawaii. The book is a fascinating account of her life as a plant biologist and gives readers an insight into the amazing world of plants. Jahren uses language that inspires and awakens curiosity. Every page conveys her own passion and enthusiasm.

Jahren starts by asking the reader to look out of the window and look for something green. If you see a leaf, she says, it is most probably a type that has been around for more than four million years. The author then asks the reader a series of questions about the leaf, before prompting the reader to ask a question of their own. Using this technique, she brings her audience into the world of plant science—because asking questions about a leaf, tree, or plant, is what plant science is all about.

Jahren goes on to tell her story—of her childhood in rural Minnesota, of her fascination with the world of plants, and her struggles in her career. She contrasts the daily routine of work in the lab—often boring and exhausting—against the moments of amazing excitement when she discovers something totally new. There are scientific descriptions of plants, trees, and flowers that are concise and easy-to-understand, and at the same time vivid and beautiful. She looks at the world from the plant's point of view and compares her own human struggle with the struggle of plants to survive. At the end of the book, she encourages her readers to plant a tree.

Credits

Photo Credits

Cover Gerd Ludwig/National Geographic Creative, **3** Kevork Djansezian/Getty Images News/Getty Images, **9** Theo Wargo/Getty Images Entertainment/Getty Images, **11** Design Pics Inc/National Geographic Creative, **12** The Asahi Shimbun/The Asahi Shimbun/Getty Images, **17** Ari Perilstein/Getty Images Entertainment/Getty Images, **19** Westend61 GmbH/Alamy Stock Photo, **20** George Leroy/Alamy Stock Photo, **25** RioPatuca/Alamy Stock Photo, **27** BSIP/Newscom, **28** Chris So/Toronto Star/Getty Images, **32** (tl) Future Music Magazine/Future/Getty Images, (tc) Maksym Bondarchuk/Shutterstock.com, (tr) Peter Kotoff/Shutterstock.com, **33** Kaspars Grinvalds/Shutterstock.com, **35** Westend61/Getty Images, **36** Bloomberg/Getty Images, **41** © Bruno Ruganzu Tusingwire, **44** Alison Hancock/Shutterstock.com, **49** © Maddalena Bearzi, **51** Tomasz Bidermann/Shutterstock.com, **52** David Parker & Julian Baum/Science Source

Text Credits

49 Adapted from "5 Simple Tips for Communicating Science": voice.nationalgeographic.com, October 2013